The Wisdom of Wallace D. Wattles

Including:

THE SCIENCE OF GETTING RICH

THE SCIENCE OF BEING GREAT

&

THE SCIENCE OF BEING WELL

© Copyright 2006 – BN Publishing

www.bnpublishing.com

info@bnpublishing.com

Printed in the U.S.A.

THE SCIENCE OF GETTING RICH

by Wallace D. Wattles

TABLE OF CONTENTS

PREFACE

THIS book is pragmatical, not philosophical; a practical manual, not a treatise upon theories. It is intended for the men and women whose most pressing need is for money; who wish to get rich first, and philosophize afterward. It is for those who have, so far, found neither the time, the means, nor the opportunity to go deeply into the study of metaphysics, but who want results and who are willing to take the conclusions of science as a basis for action, without going into all the processes by which those conclusions were reached.

It is expected that the reader will take the fundamental statements upon faith, just as he would take statements concerning a law of electrical action if they were promulgated by a Marconi or an Edison; and, taking the statements upon faith, that he will prove their truth by acting upon them without fear or hesitation. Every man or woman who does this will certainly get rich; for the science herein applied is an exact science, and failure is impossible. For the benefit, however, of those who wish to investigate philosophical theories and so secure a logical basis for faith, I will here cite certain authorities.

The monistic theory of the universe the theory that One is All, and that All is One; That one Substance manifests itself as the seeming many elements of the material world -is of Hindu origin, and has been gradually winning its way into the thought of the western world for two hundred years. It is the foundation of all the Oriental philosophies, and of those of Descartes, Spinoza, Leibnitz, Schopenhauer, Hegel, and Emerson. The reader who would dig to the philosophical foundations of this is advised to read Hegel and Emerson for himself.

In writing this book I have sacrificed all other considerations to plainness and simplicity of style, so that all might understand. The plan of action laid down therein was deduced from the conclusions of philosophy; it has been thoroughly tested, and bears the supreme test of practical experiment; it works. If you wish to know how the conclusions were arrived at, read the writings of the authors mentioned above; and if you wish to reap the fruits of their philosophies in actual practice, read this book and do exactly as it tells you to do.

The Author

CHAPTER 1

The Right to Be Rich

WHATEVER may be said in praise of poverty, the fact remains that it is not possible to live a really complete or successful life unless one is rich. No man can rise to his greatest possible height in talent or soul development unless he has plenty of money; for to unfold the soul and to develop talent he must have many things to use, and he cannot have these things unless he has money to buy them with.

A man develops in mind, soul, and body by making use of things, and society is so organized that man must have money in order to become the possessor of things; therefore, the basis of all advancement for man must be the science of getting rich.

The object of all life is development; and everything that lives has an inalienable right to all the development it is capable of attaining. Man's right to life means his right to have the free and unrestricted use of all the things which may be necessary to his fullest mental, spiritual, and physical unfoldment; or, in other words, his right to be rich.

In this book, I shall not speak of riches in a figurative way; to be really rich does not mean to be satisfied or contented with a little. No man ought to be satisfied with a little if he is capable of using and enjoying more. The purpose of Nature is the advancement and unfoldment of life; and every man should have all that can contribute to the power; elegance, beauty, and richness of life; to be content with less is sinful.

The man who owns all he wants for the living of all the life he is capable of living is rich; and no man who has not plenty of money can have all he wants. Life has advanced so far, and become so complex, that even the most ordinary man or woman requires a great amount of wealth in order to live in a manner that even approaches completeness. Every person naturally wants to become all that they are capable of becoming; this desire to realize innate possibilities is inherent in human nature; we cannot help wanting to be all that we can be. Success in life is becoming what you want to be; you can become what you want to be only by making use of things, and you can have the free use of things only as you become rich enough to buy them. To understand the science of getting rich is therefore the most essential of all knowledge.

There is nothing wrong in wanting to get rich. The desire for riches is really the desire for a richer, fuller, and more abundant life; and that desire is praise worthy. The man who does not desire to live more abundantly is abnormal, and so the man who does not desire to have money enough to by all he wants is abnormal.

There are three motives for which we live; we live for the body, we live for the mind, we live for the soul. No one of these is better or holier than the other; all are alike desirable, and no one of the three--body, mind, or soul--can live fully if either of the others is cut short of full life and expression. It is not right or noble to live only for the soul and deny mind or body; and it is wrong to live for the intellect and deny body or soul.

We are all acquainted with the loathsome consequences of living for the body and denying both mind and soul; and we see that real life means the complete expression of all that man can give forth through body, mind, and soul. Whatever he can say, no man can be really happy or satisfied unless his body is living fully in every function, and unless the same is true of his mind and his soul. Wherever there is unexpressed possibility, or function not performed, there is unsatisfied desire. Desire is possibility seeking expression, or function seeking performance.

Man cannot live fully in body without good food, comfortable clothing, and warm shelter; and without freedom from excessive toil. Rest and recreation are also necessary to his physical life. He cannot live fully in mind without books and time to study them, without opportunity for travel and observation, or without intellectual companionship. To live fully in mind he must have intellectual recreations, and must surround himself with all the objects of art and beauty he is capable of using and appreciating. To live fully in soul, man must have love; and love is denied expression by poverty.

A man's highest happiness is found in the bestowal of benefits on those he loves; love finds its most natural and spontaneous expression in giving. The man who has nothing to give cannot fill his place as a husband or father, as a citizen, or as a man. It is in the use of material things that a man finds full life for his body, develops his mind, and unfolds his soul. It is therefore of supreme importance to him that he should be rich.

It is perfectly right that you should desire to be rich; if you are a normal man or woman you cannot help doing so. It is perfectly right that you should give your best attention to the Science of Getting Rich, for it is the noblest and most necessary of all studies. If you neglect this study, you are derelict in your duty to yourself, to God and humanity; for you can render to God and humanity no greater service than to make the most of yourself.

CHAPTER 2

There is A Science of Getting Rich

THERE is a Science of getting rich, and it is an exact science, like algebra or arithmetic. There are certain laws which govern the process of acquiring riches; once these laws are learned and obeyed by any man, he will get rich with mathematical certainty.

The ownership of money and property comes as a result of doing things in a certain way; those who do things in this Certain Way, whether on purpose or accidentally, get rich; while those who do not do things in this Certain Way, no matter how hard they work or how able they are, remain poor. It is a natural law that like causes always produce like effects; and, therefore, any man or woman who learns to do things in this certain way will infallibly get rich.

That the above statement is true is shown by the following facts:
Getting rich is not a matter of environment, for, if it were, all the people in certain neighborhoods would become wealthy; the people of one city would all be rich, while those of other towns would all be poor; or the inhabitants of one state would roll in wealth, while those of an adjoining state would be in poverty.

But everywhere we see rich and poor living side by side, in the same environment, and often engaged in the same vocations. When two men are in the same locality, and in the same business, and one gets rich while the other remains poor, it shows that getting rich is not, primarily, a matter of environment. Some environments may be more favorable than others, but when two men in the same business are in the same neighborhood, and one gets rich while the other fails, it indicates that getting rich is the result of doing things in a Certain Way.

And further, the ability to do things in this certain way is not due solely to the possession of talent, for many people who have great talent remain poor, while other who have very little talent get rich. Studying the people who have got rich, we find that they are an average lot in all respects, having no greater talents and abilities than other men. It is evident that they do not get rich because they possess talents and abilities that other men have not, but because they happen to do things in a Certain Way. Getting rich is not the result of saving, or "thrift"; many very penurious people are poor, while free spenders often get rich. Nor is getting rich due to doing things which others fail to do; for two men in the same business often do almost exactly the same things, and one gets rich while the other remains poor or becomes bankrupt.

From all these things, we must come to the conclusion that getting rich is the result of doing things in a Certain Way. If getting rich is the result of doing things in a Certain Way, and if like causes always produce like effects, then any man or woman who can do things in that way can become rich, and the whole matter is brought within the domain of exact science.

The question arises here, whether this Certain Way may not be so difficult that only a few may follow it. This cannot be true, as we have seen, so far as natural ability is concerned. Talented people get rich, and blockheads get rich; intellectually brilliant people get rich, and very stupid people get rich; physically strong people get rich, and weak and sickly people get rich. Some degree of ability to think and understand is, of course, essential; but in so far natural ability is concerned, any man or woman who has sense enough to read and understand these words can certainly get rich. Also, we have seen that it is not a matter of environment. Location counts for something; one would not go to the heart of the Sahara and expect to do successful business.

Getting rich involves the necessity of dealing with men, and of being where there are people to deal with; and if these people are inclined to deal in the way you want to deal, so much the better. But that is about as far as environment goes.

If anybody else in your town can get rich, so can you; and if anybody else in your state can get rich, so can you. Again, it is not a matter of choosing some particular business or profession. People get rich in every business, and in every profession; while their next door neighbors in the same vocation remain in poverty. It is true that you will do best in a business which you like, and which is congenial to you; and if you have certain talents which are well developed, you will do best in a business which calls for the exercise of those talents. Also, you will do best in a business which is suited to your locality; an icecream parlor would do better in a warm climate than in Greenland, and a salmon fishery will succeed better in the Northwest than in Florida, where there are no salmon.

But, aside from these general limitations, getting rich is not dependent upon your engaging in some particular business, but upon your learning to do things in a Certain Way. If you are now in business, and anybody else in your locality is getting rich in the same business, while you are not getting rich, it is because you are not doing things in the same Way that the other person is doing them. No one is prevented from getting rich by lack of capital. True, as you get capital the increase becomes more easy and rapid; but one who has capital is already rich, and does not need to consider how to become so.

No matter how poor you may be, if you begin to do things in the Certain Way you will begin to get rich; and you will begin to have capital. The getting of capital is a part of the process of getting rich; and it is a part of the result which invariably follows the doing of things in the Certain Way. You may be the poorest man on the continent, and be deeply in debt; you may have neither friends, influence, nor resources; but if you begin to do things in this way, you must infallibly begin to get rich, for like causes must produce like effects. If you have no capital, you can get capital; if you are in the wrong business, you can get into the right business; if you are in the wrong location, you can go to the right location; and you can do so by beginning in your present business and in your present location to do things in the Certain Way which causes success.

CHAPTER 3

Is Opportunity Monopolized?

NO man is kept poor because opportunity has been taken away from him; because other people have monopolized the wealth, and have put a fence around it. You may be shut off from engaging in business in certain lines, but there are other channels open to you. Probably it would be hard for you to get control of any of the great railroad systems; that field is pretty well monopolized. But the electric railway business is still in its infancy, and offers plenty of scope for enterprise; and it will be but a very few years until traffic and transportation through the air will become a great industry, and in all its branches will give employment to hundreds of thousands, and perhaps to millions, of people. Why not turn your attention to the development of aerial transportation, instead of competing with J.J. Hill and others for a chance in the steam railway world?

It is quite true that if you are a workman in the employ of the steel trust you have very little chance of becoming the owner of the plant in which you work; but it is also true that if you will commence to act in a Certain Way, you can soon leave the employ of the steel trust; you can buy a farm of from ten to forty acres, and engage in business as a producer of foodstuffs. There is great opportunity at this time for men who will live upon small tracts of land and cultivate the same intensively; such men will certainly get rich. You may say that it is impossible for you to get the land, but I am going to prove to you that it is not impossible, and that you can certainly get a farm if you will go to work in a Certain Way.

At different periods the tide of opportunity sets in different directions, according to the needs of the whole, and the particular stage of social evolution which has been reached. At present, in America, it is setting toward agriculture and the allied industries and professions. Today, opportunity is open before the factory worker in his line. It is open before the business man who supplies the farmer more than before the one who supplies the factory worker; and before the professional man who waits upon the farmer more than before the one who serves the working class. There is abundance of opportunity for the man who will go with the tide, instead of trying to swim against it.

So the factory workers, either as individuals or as a class, are not deprived of opportunity. The workers are not being "kept down" by their masters; they are not being "ground" by the trusts and combinations of capital. As a class, they are where they are because they do not do things in a Certain Way. If the workers of America chose to do so, they could follow the example of their brothers in Belgium and other countries, and establish great department stores and co-operative industries; they could elect men of their own class to office, and pass laws favoring the development of such co-operative industries; and in a few years they could take peaceable possession of the industrial field.

The working class may become the master class whenever they will begin to do things in a Certain Way; the law of wealth is the same for them as it is for all others. This they must learn; and they will remain where they are as long as they continue to do as they do. The individual worker, however, is not held down by the ignorance or the mental slothfulness of his class; he can follow the tide of opportunity to riches, and this book will tell him how.

No one is kept in poverty by shortness in the supply of riches; there is more than enough for all. A palace as large as the capitol at Washington might be built for every family on earth from the building material in the United States alone; and under intensive cultivation, this country would produce wool, cotton, linen, and silk enough to cloth each person in the world finer than Solomon was arrayed in all his glory; together with food enough to feed them all luxuriously.

The visible supply is practically inexhaustible; and the invisible supply really IS inexhaustible. Everything you see on earth is made from one original substance, out of which all things proceed. New Forms are constantly being made, and older ones are dissolving; but all are shapes assumed by One Thing. There is no limit to the supply of Formless Stuff, or Original Substance. The universe is made out of it; but it was not all used in making the universe. The spaces in, through, and between the forms of the visible universe are permeated and filled with the Original Substance; with the formless Stuff; with the raw material of all things. Ten thousand times as much as has been made might still be made, and even then we should not have exhausted the supply of universal raw material.

No man, therefore, is poor because nature is poor, or because there is not enough to go around. Nature is an inexhaustible storehouse of riches; the supply will never run short. Original Substance is alive with creative energy, and is constantly producingmore forms. When the supply of building material is exhausted, more will be produced; when the soil is exhausted so that food stuffs and materials for Clothing will no longer grow upon it, it will be renewed or more soil will be made. When all the gold and silver has been dug from the earth, if man is still in such a stage of social development that he needs gold and silver, more will produced from the Formless. The Formless Stuff responds to the needs of man; it will not let him be without any good thing.
This is true of man collectively; the race as a whole is always abundantly rich, and if individuals are poor, it is because they do not follow the Certain Way of doing things which makes the individual man rich. The Formless Stuff is intelligent; it is stuff which thinks. It is alive, and is always impelled toward more life.

It is the natural and inherent impulse of life to seek to live more; it is the nature of intelligence to enlarge itself, and of consciousness to seek to extend its boundaries and find fuller expression. The universe of forms has been made by Formless Living Substance, throwing itself into form in order to express itself more fully. The universe is a great Living Presence, always moving inherently toward more life and fuller functioning. Nature is formed for the advancement of life; its impelling motive is the increase of life. For this cause, everything which can possibly minister to life is bountifully provided; there can be no lack unless God is to contradict himself and nullify his own works.

You are not kept poor by lack in the supply of riches; it is a fact which I shall demonstrate a little farther on that even the resources of the Formless Supply are at the command of the man or woman will act and think in a Certain Way.

CHAPTER 4

The First Principle in The Science of Getting Rich

THOUGHT is the only power which can produce tangible riches from the Formless Substance. The stuff from which all things are made is a substance which thinks, and a thought of form in this substance produces the form. Original Substance moves according to its thoughts; every form and process you see in nature is the visible expression of a thought in Original Substance. As the Formless Stuff thinks of a form, it takes that form; as it thinks of a motion, it makes that motion. That is the way all things were created. We live in a thought world, which is part of a thought universe. The thought of a moving universe extended throughout Formless Substance, and the Thinking Stuff moving according to that thought, took the form of systems of planets, and maintains that form. Thinking Substance takes the form of its thought, and moves according to the thought.

Holding the idea of a circling system of suns and worlds, it takes the form of these bodies, and moves them as it thinks. Thinking the form of a slow-growing oak tree, it moves accordingly, and produces the tree, though centuries may be required to do the work. In creating, the Formless seems to move according to the lines of motion it has established; the thought of an oak tree does not cause the instant formation of a full-grown tree, but it does start in motion the forces which will produce the tree, along established lines of growth. Every thought of form, held in thinking Substance, causes the creation of the form, but always, or at least generally, along lines of growth and action already established.

The thought of a house of a certain construction, if it were impressed upon Formless Substance, might not cause the instant formation, of the house; but it would cause the turning of creative energies already working in trade and commerce into such channels as to result in the speedy building of the house. And if there were no existing channels through which the creative energy could work, then the house would be formed directly from primal substance, without waiting for the slow processes of the organic and inorganic world. No thought of form can be impressed upon Original Substance without causing the creation of the form.

Man is a thinking center, and can originate thought. All the forms that man fashions with his hands must first exist in his thought; he cannot shape a thing until he has thought that thing. And so far man has confined his efforts wholly to the work of his hands; he has applied manual labor to the world of forms, seeking to change or modify those already existing. He has never thought of trying to cause the creation of new forms by impressing his thoughts upon Formless Substance. When man has a thought-form, he takes material from the forms of nature, and makes an image of the form which is in his mind. He has, so far, made little or no effort to co-operate with Formless Intelligence; to work "with the Father." He has not dreamed that he can "do what he seeth the Father doing." Man reshapes and modifies existing forms by manual labor; he has given no attention to the question whether he may not produce things from Formless Substance by communicating his thoughts to it. We propose to prove that he may do so; to prove that any man or woman may do so, and to show how.

As our first step, we must lay down three fundamental propositions.

First, we assert that there is one original formless stuff, or substance, from which all things are made. All the seemingly many elements are but different presentations of one element; all the many forms found in organic and inorganic nature are but different shapes, made from the same stuff. And this stuff is thinking stuff; a thought held in it produces the form of the thought. Thought, in thinking substance, produces shapes. Man is a thinking center, capable of original thought; if man can communicate his thought to original thinking substance, he can cause the creation, or formation, of the thing he thinks about.

To summarize this:
There is a thinking stuff from which all things are made, and which, in its original state, permeates, penetrates, and fills the interspaces of the universe. A thought, in this substance, produces the thing that is imaged by the thought. Man can form things in his thought, and, by impressing his thought upon formless substance, can cause the thing he thinks about to be created.

It may be asked if I can prove these statements; and without going into details, I answer that I can do so, both by logic and experience. Reasoning back from the phenomena of form and thought, I come to one original thinking substance; and reasoning forward from this thinking substance, I come to man's power to cause the formation of the thing he thinks about.

And by experiment, I find the reasoning true; and this is my strongest proof. If one man who reads this book gets rich by doing what it tells him to do, that is evidence in support of my claim; but if every man who does what it tells him to do gets rich, that is positive proof until some one goes through the process and fails. The theory is true until the process fails; and this process will not fail, for every man who does exactly what this book tells him to do will get rich.

I have said that men get rich by doing things in a Certain Way; and in order to do so, men must become able to think in a certain way. A man's way of doing things is the direct result of the way he thinks about things. To do things in a way you want to do them, you will have to acquire the ability to think the way you want to think; this is the first step toward getting rich. To think what you want to think is to think TRUTH, regardless of appearances. Every man has the natural and inherent power to think what he wants to think, but it requires far more effort to do so than it does to think the thoughts which are suggested by appearances. To think according to appearance is easy; to think truth regardless of appearances is laborious, and requires the expenditure of more power than any other workman is called upon to perform.

There is no labor from which most people shrink as they do from that of sustained and consecutive thought; it is the hardest work in the world. This is especially true when truth is contrary to appearances. Every appearance in the visible world tends to produce a corresponding form in the mind which observes it; and this can only be prevented by holding the thought of the TRUTH.

To look upon the appearance of disease will produce the form of disease in your own mind, and ultimately in your body, unless you hold the thought of the truth, which is that there is no disease; it is only an appearance, and the reality is health. To look upon the appearances of poverty will produce corresponding forms in your own mind, unless you hold to the truth that there is no poverty; there is only abundance. To think health when surrounded by the appearances of disease, or to think riches when in the midst of appearances of poverty, requires power; but he who acquires this power becomes a MASTER MIND. He can conquer fate; he can have what he wants.

This power can only be acquired by getting hold of the basic fact which is behind all appearances; and that fact is that there is one Thinking Substance, from which and by which all things are made. Then we must grasp the truth that every thought held in this substance becomes a form, and that man can so impress his thoughts upon it as to cause them to take form and become visible things.

When we realize this, we lose all doubt and fear, for we know that we can create what we want to create; we can get what we want to have, and can become what we want to be. As a first step toward getting rich, you must believe the three fundamental statements given previously in this chapter; and in order to emphasize them. I repeat them here:
There is a thinking stuff from which all things are made, and which, in its original state, permeates, penetrates, and fills the interspaces of the universe. A thought, in this substance, Produces the thing that is imaged by the thought. Man can form things in his thought, and, by impressing his thought upon formless substance, can cause the thing he thinks about to be created. You must lay aside all other concepts of the universe than this monistic one; and you must dwell upon this until it is fixed in your mind, and has become your habitual thought.

Read these creed statements over and over again; fix every word upon your memory, and meditate upon them until you firmly believe what they say. If a doubt comes to you, cast it aside as a sin. Do not listen to arguments against this idea; do not go to churches or lectures where a contrary concept of things is taught or preached. Do not read magazines or books which teach a different idea; if you get mixed up in your faith, all your efforts will be in vain. Do not ask why these things are true, nor speculate as to how they can be true; simply take them on trust. The science of getting rich begins with the absolute acceptance of this faith.

CHAPTER 5

Increasing Life

YOU must get rid of the last vestige of the old idea that there is a Deity whose will it is that you should be poor, or whose purposes may be served by keeping you in poverty. The Intelligent Substance which is All, and in All, and which lives in All and lives in you, is a consciously Living Substance. Being a consciously living substance, It must have the nature and inherent desire of every living intelligence for increase of life. Every living thing must continually seek for the enlargement of its life, because life, in the mere act of living, must increase itself.

A seed, dropped into the ground, springs into activity, and in the act of living produces a hundred more seeds; life, by living, multiplies itself. It is forever becoming More; it must do so, if it continues to be at all. Intelligence is under this same necessity for continuous increase. Every thought we think makes it necessary for us to think another thought; consciousness is continually expanding. Every fact we learn leads us to the learning of another fact; knowledge is continually increasing. Every talent we cultivate brings to the mind the desire to cultivate another talent; we are subject to the urge of life, seeking expression, which ever drives us on to know more, to do more, and to be more.

In order to know more, do more, and be more we must have more; we must have things to use, for we learn, and do, and become, only by using things. We must get rich, so that we can live more.

The desire for riches is simply the capacity for larger life seeking fulfillment; every desire is the effort of an unexpressed possibility to come into action. It is power seeking to manifest which causes desire. That which makes you want more money is the same as that which makes the plant grow; it is Life, seeking fuller expression.

The One Living Substance must be subject to this inherent law of all life; it is permeated with the desire to live more; that is why it is under the necessity of creating things. The One Substance desires to live more in you; hence it wants you to have all the things you can use. It is the desire of God that you should get rich. He wants you to get rich because he can express himself better through you if you have plenty of things to use in giving him expression. He can live more in you if you have unlimited command of the means of life.

The universe desires you to have everything you want to have. Nature is friendly to your plans. Everything is naturally for you. Make up your mind that this is true. It is essential, however that your purpose should harmonize with the purpose that is in All. You must want real life, not mere pleasure of sensual gratification. Life is the performance of function; and the individual really lives only when he performs every function, physical, mental, and spiritual, of which he is capable, without excess in any.

You do not want to get rich in order to live swinishly, for the gratification of animal desires; that is not life. But the performance of every physical function is a part of life, and no one lives completely who denies the impulses of the body a normal and healthful expression. You do not want to get rich solely to enjoy mental pleasures, to get knowledge, to gratify ambition, to outshine others, to be famous. All these are a legitimate part of life, but the man who lives for the pleasures of the intellect alone will only have a partial life, and he will never be satisfied with his lot. You do not want to get rich solely for the good of others, to lose yourself for the salvation of mankind, to experience the joys of philanthropy and sacrifice. The joys of the soul are only a part of life; and they are no better or nobler than any other part.

You want to get rich in order that you may eat, drink, and be merry when it is time to do these things; in order that you may surround yourself with beautiful things, see distant lands, feed your mind, and develop your intellect; in order that you may love men and do kind things, and be able to play a good part in helping the world to find truth.

But remember that extreme altruism is no better and no nobler than extreme selfishness; both are mistakes. Get rid of the idea that God wants you to sacrifice yourself for others, and that you can secure his favor by doing so; God requires nothing of the kind. What he wants is that you should make the most of yourself, for yourself, and for others; and you can help others more by making the most of yourself than in any other way. You can make the most of yourself only by getting rich; so it is right and praiseworthy that you should give your first and best thought to the work of acquiring wealth.

Remember, however, that the desire of Substance is for all, and its movements must be for more life to all; it cannot be made to work for less life to any, because it is equally in all, seeking riches and life. Intelligent Substance will make things for you, but it will not take things away from some one else and give them to you. You must get rid of the thought of competition. You are to create, not to compete for what is already created. You do not have to take anything away from any one. You do not have to drive sharp bargains. You do not have to cheat, or to take advantage. You do not need to let any man work for you for less than he earns. You do not have to covet the property of others, or to look at it with wishful eyes; no man has anything of which you cannot have the like, and that without taking what he has away from him. You are to become a creator, not a competitor; you are going to get what you want, but in such a way that when you get it every other man will have more than he has now.

I am aware that there are men who get a vast amount of money by proceeding in direct opposition to the statements in the paragraph above, and may add a word of explanation here. Men of the plutocratic type, who become very rich, do so sometimes purely by their extraordinary ability on the plane of competition; and sometimes they unconsciously relate themselves to Substance in its great purposes and movements for the general racial upbuilding through industrial evolution. Rockefeller, Carnegie, Morgan, et al., have been the unconscious agents of the

19

Supreme in the necessary work of systematizing and organizing productive industry; and in the end, their work will contribute immensely toward increased life for all.

Their day is nearly over; they have organized production, and will soon be succeeded by the agents of the multitude, who will organize the machinery of distribution. The multi-millionaires are like the monster reptiles of the prehistoric eras; they play a necessary part in the evolutionary process, but the same Power which produced them will dispose of them. And it is well to bear in mind that they have never been really rich; a record of the private lives of most of this class will show that they have really been the most abject and wretched of the poor. Riches secured on the competitive plane are never satisfactory and permanent; they are yours today, and another's tomorrow.

Remember, if you are to become rich in a scientific and certain way, you must rise entirely out of the competitive thought. You must never think for a moment that the supply is limited. Just as soon as you begin to think that all the money is being "cornered" and controlled by bankers and others, and that you must exert yourself to get laws passed to stop this process, and so on; in that moment you drop into the competitive mind, and your power to cause creation is gone for the time being; and what is worse, you will probably arrest the creative movements you have already instituted.

KNOW that there are countless millions of dollars' worth of gold in the mountains of the earth, not yet brought to light; and know that if there were not, more would be created from Thinking Substance to supply your needs. KNOW that the money you need will come, even if it is necessary for a thousand men to be led to the discovery of new gold mines to-morrow. Never look at the visible supply; look always at the limitless riches in Formless Substance, and KNOW that they are coming to you as fast as you can receive and use them. Nobody, by cornering the visible supply, can prevent you from getting what is yours.

So never allow yourself to think for an instant that all the best building spots will be taken before you get ready to build your house, unless you hurry. Never worry about the trusts and combines, and get anxious for fear they will soon come to own the whole earth. Never get afraid that you will lose what you want because some other person "beats you to it." That cannot possibly happen; you are not seeking any thing that is possessed by anybody else; you are causing what you want to be created from formless Substance, and the supply is without limits.

Stick to the formulated statement:
There is a thinking stuff from which all things are made, and which, in its original state, permeates, penetrates, and fills the interspaces of the universe. A thought, in this substance, produces the thing that is imaged by the thought. Man can form things in his thought, and, by impressing his thought upon formless substance, can cause the thing he thinks about to be created.

CHAPTER 6

How Riches Come to You

WHEN I say that you do not have to drive sharp bargains, I do not mean that you do not have to drive any bargains at all, or that you are above the necessity for having any dealings with your fellow men. I mean that you will not need to deal with them unfairly; you do not have to get something for nothing, but can give to every man more than you take from him.

You cannot give every man more in cash market value than you take from him, but you can give him more in use value than the cash value of the thing you take from him. The paper, ink, and other material in this book may not be worth the money you pay for it; but if the ideas suggested by it bring you thousands of dollars, you have not been wronged by those who sold it to you; they have given you a great use value for a small cash value.

Let us suppose that I own a picture by one of the great artists, which, in any civilized community, is worth thousands of dollars. I take it to Baffin Ray, and by "salesmanship" induce an Eskimo to give a bundle of furs worth $ 500 for it. I have really wronged him, for he has no use for the picture; it has no use value to him; it will not add to his life. But suppose I give him a gun worth $50 for his furs; then he has made a good bargain. He has use for the gun; it will get him many more furs and much food; it will add to his life in every way; it will make him rich.

When you rise from the competitive to the creative plane, you can scan your business transactions very strictly, and if you are selling any man anything which does not add more to his life than the thing he give you in exchange, you can afford to stop it. You do not have to beat anybody in business. And if you are in a business which does beat people, get out of it at once. Give every man more in use value than you take from him in cash value; then you are adding to the life of the world by every business transaction. If you have people working for you, you must take from them more in cash value than you pay them in wages; but you can so organize your business that it will be filled with the principle of advancement, and so that each employee who wishes to do so may advance a little every day. You can make your business do for your employees what this book is doing for you. You can so conduct your business that it will be a sort of ladder, by which every employee who will take the trouble may climb to riches himself; and given the opportunity, if he will not do so it is not your fault.

And finally, because you are to cause the creation of your riches from Formless Substance which permeates all your environment, it does not follow that they are to take shape from the atmosphere and come into being before your eyes. If you want a sewing machine, for instance, I do not mean to tell you that you are to impress the thought of a sewing machine on Thinking Substance until the machine is formed without hands, in the room where you sit, or elsewhere. But if you want a sewing machine, hold the mental image of it with the most positive certainty that it is being made, or is on its way to you. After once forming the thought, have the most absolute and unquestioning faith that the sewing machine is coming; never think of it, or speak, of it, in any other way than as being sure to arrive. Claim it as already yours.

It will be brought to you by the power of the Supreme Intelligence, acting upon the minds of men. If you live in Maine, it may be that a man will be brought from Texas or Japan to engage in some transaction which will result in your getting what you want. If so, the whole matter will be as much to that man's advantage as it is to yours.

Do not forget for a moment that the Thinking Substance is through all, in all, communicating with all, and can influence all. The desire of Thinking Substance for fuller life and better living has caused the creation of all the sewing machines already made; and it can cause the creation of millions more, and will, whenever men set it in motion by desire and faith, and by acting in a Certain Way.

You can certainly have a sewing machine in your house; and it is just as certain that you can have any other thing or things which you want, and which you will use for the advancement of your own life and the lives of others.

You need not hesitate about asking largely. Original Substance wants to live all that is possible in you, and wants you to have all that you can or will use for the living of the most abundant life. If you fix upon your consciousness the fact that the desire you feel for the possession of riches is one with the desire of Omnipotence for more complete expression, your faith becomes invincible.

Once I saw a little boy sitting at a piano, and vainly trying to bring harmony out of the keys; and I saw that he was grieved and provoked by his inability to play real music. I asked him the cause of his vexation, and he answered, "I can feel the music in me, but I can't make my hands go right." The music in him was the URGE of Original Substance, containing all the possibilities of all life; all that there is of music was seeking expression through the child.

God, the One Substance, is trying to live and do and enjoy things through humanity. He is saying "I want hands to build wonderful structures, to play divine harmonies, to paint glorious pictures; I want feet to run my errands, eyes to see my beauties, tongues to tell mighty truths and to sing marvelous songs," and so on. All that there is of possibility is seeking expression through men. God wants those who can play music to have pianos and every other instrument, and to have the means to cultivate their talents to the fullest extent; He wants those who can appreciate beauty to be able to surround themselves with beautiful things; He wants those who can discern truth to have every opportunity to travel and observe; He wants those who can appreciate dress to be beautifully clothed, and those who can appreciate good food to be luxuriously fed. He wants all these things because it is Himself that enjoys and appreciates them; it is God who wants to play, and sing, and enjoy beauty, and proclaim truth and wear fine clothes, and eat good foods. "It is God that worketh in you to will and to do," said Paul.

The desire you feel for riches is the infinite, seeking to express Himself in you as He sought to find expression in the little boy at the piano. So you need not hesitate to ask largely. Your part is to focalize and express the desire to God.

This is a difficult point with most people; they retain something of the old idea that poverty and self-sacrifice are pleasing to God. They look upon poverty as a part of the plan, a necessity of nature. They have the idea that God has finished His work, and made all that He can make, and that the majority of men must stay poor because there is not enough to go around. They hold to so much of this erroneous thought that they feel ashamed to ask for wealth; they try not to want more than a very modest competence, just enough to make them fairly comfortable.

I recall now the case of one student who was told that he must get in mind a clear picture of the things he desired, so that the creative thought of them might be impressed on Formless Substance. He was a very poor man, living in a rented house, and having only what he earned from day to day; and he could not grasp the fact that all wealth was his. So, after thinking the matter over, he decided that he might reasonably ask for a new rug for the floor of his best room, and an anthracite coal stove to heat the house during the cold weather. Following the instructions given in this book, he obtained these things in a few months; and then it dawned upon him that he had not asked enough. He went through the house in which he lived, and planned all the improvements he would like to make in it; he mentally added a bay window here and a room there, until it was complete in his mind as his ideal home; and then he planned its furnishings.

Holding the whole picture in his mind, he began living in the Certain Way, and moving toward what he wanted; and he owns the house now, and is rebuilding it after the form of his mental image. And now, with still larger faith, he is going on to get greater things. It has been unto him according to his faith, and it is so with you and with all of us.

CHAPTER 7

Gratitude

THE illustrations given in the last chapter will have conveyed to the reader the fact that the first step toward getting rich is to convey the idea of your wants to the Formless Substance. This is true, and you will see that in order to do so it becomes necessary to relate yourself to the Formless Intelligence in a harmonious way. To secure this harmonious relation is a matter of such primary and vital importance that I shall give some space to its discussion here, and give you instructions which, if you will follow them, will be certain to bring you into perfect unity of mind with God.

The whole process of mental adjustment and atonement can be summed up in one word, gratitude.

First, you believe that there is one Intelligent Substance, from which all things proceed; second, you believe that this Substance gives you everything you desire; and third, you relate yourself to it by a feeling of deep and profound gratitude.

Many people who order their lives rightly in all other ways are kept in poverty by their lack of gratitude. Having received one gift from God, they cut the wires which connect them with Him by failing to make acknowledgment. It is easy to understand that the nearer we live to the source of wealth, the more wealth we shall receive; and it is easy also to understand that the soul that is always grateful lives in closer touch with God than the one which never looks to Him in thankful acknowledgment.

The more gratefully we fix our minds on the Supreme when good things come to us, the more good things we will receive, and the more rapidly they will come; and the reason simply is that the mental attitude of gratitude draws the mind into closer touch with the source from which the blessings come. If it is a new thought to you that gratitude brings your whole mind into closer harmony with the creative energies of the universe, consider it well, and you will see that it is true. The good things you already have have come to you along the line of obedience to certain laws. Gratitude will lead your mind out along the ways by which things come; and it will keep you in close harmony with creative thought and prevent you from falling into competitive thought. Gratitude alone can keep you looking toward the All, and prevent you from falling into the error of thinking of the supply as limited; and to do that would be fatal to your hopes.

There is a Law of Gratitude, and it is absolutely necessary that you should observe the law, if you are to get the results you seek. The law of gratitude is the natural principle that action and reaction are always equal, and in opposite directions. The grateful outreaching of your mind in thankful praise to the Supreme is a liberation or expenditure of force; it cannot fail to reach that to which it addressed, and the reaction is an instantaneous movement towards you. "Draw nigh unto God, and He will draw nigh unto you." That is a statement of psychological truth.

And if your gratitude is strong and constant, the reaction in Formless Substance will be strong and continuous; the movement of the things you want will be always toward you. You cannot exercise much power without gratitude; for it is gratitude that keeps you connected with Power. But the value of gratitude does not consist solely in getting you more blessings in the future. Without gratitude you cannot long keep from dissatisfied thought regarding things as they are.

The moment you permit your mind to dwell with dissatisfaction upon things as they are, you begin to lose ground. You fix attention upon the common, the ordinary, the poor, and the squalid and mean; and your mind takes the form of these things. Then you will transmit these forms or mental images to the Formless, and the common, the poor, the squalid, and mean will come to you. To permit your mind to dwell upon the inferior is to become inferior and to surround yourself with inferior things. On the other hand, to fix your attention on the best is to surround yourself with the best, and to become the best.

The Creative Power within us makes us into the image of that to which we give our attention. We are Thinking Substance, and thinking substance always takes the form of that which it thinks about. The grateful mind is constantly fixed upon the best; therefore it tends to become the best; it takes the form or character of the best, and will receive the best.

Also, faith is born of gratitude. The grateful mind continually expects good things, and expectation becomes faith. The reaction of gratitude upon one's own mind produces faith; and every outgoing wave of grateful thanksgiving increases faith. He who has no feeling of gratitude cannot long retain a living faith; and without a living faith you cannot get rich by the creative method, as we shall see in the following chapters.

It is necessary, then, to cultivate the habit of being grateful for every good thing that comes to you; and to give thanks continuously. And because all things have contributed to your advancement, you should include all things in your gratitude. Do not waste time thinking or talking about the shortcomings or wrong actions of plutocrats or trust magnates. Their organization of the world has made your opportunity; all you get really comes to you because of them. Do not rage against, corrupt politicians; if it were not for politicians we should fall into anarchy, and your opportunity would be greatly lessened.

God has worked a long time and very patiently to bring us up to where we are in industry and government, and He is going right on with His work. There is not the least doubt that He will do away with plutocrats, trust magnates, captains of industry, and politicians as soon as they can be spared; but in the meantime, behold they are all very good. Remember that they are all helping to arrange the lines of transmission along which your riches will come to you, and be grateful to them all.

This will bring you into harmonious relations with the good in everything, and the good in everything will move toward you.

CHAPTER 8

Thinking in the Certain Way

TURN back to chapter 6 and read again the story of the man who formed a mental image of his house, and you will get a fair idea of the initial step toward getting rich. You must form a clear and definite mental picture of what you want; you cannot transmit an idea unless you have it yourself. You must have it before you can give it; and many people fail to impress Thinking Substance because they have themselves only a vague and misty concept of the things they want to do, to have, or to become.

It is not enough that you should have a general desire for wealth "to do good with"; everybody has that desire. It is not enough that you should have a wish to travel, see things, live more, etc. Everybody has those desires also. If you were going to send a wireless message to a friend, you would not send the letters of the alphabet in their order, and let him construct the message for himself; nor would you take words at random from the dictionary. You would send a coherent sentence; one which meant something. When you try to impress your wants upon Substance, remember that it must be done by a coherent statement; you must know what you want, and be definite. You can never get rich, or start the creative power into action, by sending out unformed longings and vague desires.

Go over your desires just as the man I have described went over his house; see just what you want, and get a clear mental picture of it as you wish it to look when you get it. That clear mental picture you must have continually in mind, as the sailor has in mind the port toward which he is sailing the ship; you must keep your face toward it all the time. You must no more lose sight of it than the steersman loses sight of the compass.

It is not necessary to take exercises in concentration, nor to set apart special times for prayer and affirmation, nor to "go into the silence," nor to do occult stunts of any kind. There things are well enough, but all you need is to know what you want, and to want it badly enough so that it will stay in your thoughts. Spend as much of your leisure time as you can in contemplating your picture, but no one needs to take exercises to concentrate his mind on a thing which he really wants; it is the things you do not really care about which require effort to fix your attention upon them.

And unless you really want to get rich, so that the desire is strong enough to hold your thoughts directed to the purpose as the magnetic pole holds the needle of the compass, it will hardly be worth while for you to try to carry out the instructions given in this book. The methods herein set forth are for people whose desire for riches is strong enough to overcome mental laziness and the love of ease, and make them work.

The more clear and definite you make your picture then, and the more you dwell upon it, bringing out all its delightful details, the stronger your desire will be; and the stronger your desire, the easier it will be to hold your mind fixed upon the picture of what you want.

Something more is necessary, however, than merely to see the picture clearly. If that is all you do, you are only a dreamer, and will have little or no power for accomplishment. Behind your clear vision must be the purpose to realize it; to bring it out in tangible expression. And behind this purpose must be an invincible and unwavering FAITH that the thing is already yours; that it is "at hand" and you have only to take possession of it.

Live in the new house, mentally, until it takes form around you physically. In the mental realm, enter at once into full enjoyment of the things you want. See the things you want as if they were actually around you all the time; see yourself as owning and using them. Make use of them in imagination just as you will use them when they are your tangible possessions. Dwell upon your mental picture until it is clear and distinct, and then take the Mental Attitude of Ownership toward everything in that picture. Take possession of it, in mind, in the full faith that it is actually yours. Hold to this mental ownership; do not waiver for an instant in the faith that it is real.

And remember what was said in a proceeding chapter about gratitude; be as thankful for it all the time as you expect to be when it has taken form. The man who can sincerely thank God for the things which as yet he owns only in imagination, has real faith. He will get rich; he will cause the creation of whatsoever he wants. You do not need to pray repeatedly for things you want; it is not necessary to tell God about it every day. Your part is to intelligently formulate your desire for the things which make for a larger life, and to get these desire arranged into a coherent whole; and then to impress this Whole Desire upon the Formless Substance, which has the power and the will to bring you what you want.

You do not make this impression by repeating strings of words; you make it by holding the vision with unshakable PURPOSE to attain it, and with steadfast FAITH that you do attain it. The answer to prayer is not according to your faith while you are talking, but according to your faith while you are working. You cannot impress the mind of God by having a special Sabbath day set apart to tell Him what you want, and the forgetting Him during the rest of the week. You cannot impress Him by having special hours to go into your closet and pray, if you then dismiss the matter from your mind until the hour of prayer comes again.

Oral prayer is well enough, and has its effect, especially upon yourself, in clarifying your vision and strengthening your faith; but it is not your oral petitions which get you what you want. In order to get rich you do not need a "sweet hour of prayer"; you need to "pray without ceasing." And by prayer I mean holding steadily to your vision, with the purpose to cause its creation into solid form, and the faith that you are doing so. "Believe that ye receive them."

The whole matter turns on receiving, once you have clearly formed your vision. When you have formed it, it is well to make an oral statement, addressing the Supreme in reverent prayer; and from that moment you must, in mind, receive what you ask for. Live in the new house; wear the fine clothes; ride in the automobile; go on the journey, and confidently plan for greater journeys. Think and speak of all the things you have asked for in terms of actual present ownership. Imagine an environment, and a financial condition exactly as you want them, and live all the time in that imaginary environment and financial condition.

Mind, however, that you do not do this as a mere dreamer and castle builder; hold to the FAITH that the imaginary is being realized, and to the PURPOSE to realize it. Remember that it is faith and purpose in the use of the imagination which make the difference between the scientist and the dreamer. And having learned this fact, it is here that you must learn the proper use of the Will.

CHAPTER 9

How to Use the Will

TO set about getting rich in a scientific way, you do not try to apply your will power to anything outside of yourself. Your have no right to do so, anyway. It is wrong to apply your will to other men and women, in order to get them to do what you wish done.

It is as flagrantly wrong to coerce people by mental power as it is to coerce them by physical power. If compelling people by physical force to do things for you reduces them to slavery, compelling them by mental means accomplishes exactly the same thing; the only difference is in methods. If taking things from people by physical force is robbery, then taking things by mental force is robbery also; there is no difference in principle. You have no right to use your will power upon another person, even "for his own good"; for you do not know what is for his good. The science of getting rich does not require you to apply power or force to any other person, in any way whatsoever. There is not the slightest necessity for doing so; indeed, any attempt to use your will upon others will only tend to defeat your purpose. You do not need to apply your will to things, in order to compel them to come to you.

That would simply be trying to coerce God, and would be foolish and useless, as well as irreverent. You do not have to compel God to give you good things, any more than you have to use your will power to make the sun rise. You do not have to use your will power to conquer an unfriendly deity, or to make stubborn and rebellious forces do your bidding. Substance is friendly to you, and is more anxious to give you what you want than you are to get it. To get rich, you need only to use your will power upon yourself.

When you know what to think and do, then you must use your will to compel yourself to think and do the right things. That is the legitimate use of the will in getting what you want--to use it in holding yourself to the right course. Use your will to keep yourself thinking and acting in the Certain Way. Do not try to project your will, or your thoughts, or your mind out into space, to "act" on things or people. Keep your mind at home; it can accomplish more there than elsewhere. Use your mind to form a mental image of what you want, and to hold that vision with faith and purpose; and use your will to keep your mind working in the Right Way.

The more steady and continuous your faith and purpose, the more rapidly you will get rich, because you will make only POSITIVE impressions upon Substance; and you will not neutralize or offset them by negative impressions. The picture of your desires, held with faith and purpose, is taken up by the Formless, and permeates it to great distances-throughout the universe, for all I know.

As this impression spreads, all things are set moving toward its realization; every living thing, every inanimate thing, and the things yet uncreated, are stirred toward bringing into being that which you want. All force begins to be exerted in that direction; all things begin to move toward you. The minds of people, everywhere, are influenced toward doing the things necessary to the fulfilling of your desires; and they work for you, unconsciously.

But you can check all this by starting a negative impression in the Formless Substance. Doubt or unbelief is as certain to start a movement away from you as faith and purpose are to start one toward you. It is by not understanding this that most people who try to make use of "mental science" in getting rich make their failure. Every hour and moment you spend in giving heed to doubts and fears, every hour you spend in worry, every hour in which your soul is possessed by unbelief, sets a current away from you in the whole domain of intelligent Substance. All the promises are unto them that believe, and unto them only.

Since belief is all important, it behooves you to guard your thoughts; and as your beliefs will be shaped to a very great extent by the things you observe and think about, it is important that you should command your attention. And here the will comes into use; for it is by your will that you determine upon what things your attention shall be fixed.

If you want to become rich, you must not make a study of poverty. Things are not brought into being by thinking about their opposites. Health is never to be attained by studying disease and thinking about disease; righteousness is not to be promoted by studying sin and thinking about sin; and no one ever got rich by studying poverty and thinking about poverty. Medicine as a science of disease has increased disease; religion as a science of sin has promoted sin, and economics as a study of poverty will fill the world with wretchedness and want.

Do not talk about poverty; do not investigate it, or concern yourself with it. Never mind what its causes are; you have nothing to do with them. What concerns you is the cure. Do not spend your time in charitable work, or charity movements; all charity only tends to perpetuate the wretchedness it aims to eradicate. I do not say that you should be hard hearted or unkind, and refuse to hear the cry of need; but you must not try to eradicate poverty in any of the conventional ways. Put poverty behind you, and put all that pertains to it behind you, and "make good." Get rich; that is the best way you can help the poor.

And you cannot hold the mental image which is to make you rich if you fill your mind with pictures of poverty. Do not read books or papers which give circumstantial accounts of the wretchedness of the tenement dwellers, of the horrors of child labor, and so on. Do not read anything which fills your mind with gloomy images of want and suffering. You cannot help the poor in the least by knowing about these things; and the wide-spread knowledge of them does not tend at all to do away with poverty. What tends to do away with poverty is not the getting of pictures of poverty into your mind, but getting pictures of wealth into the minds of the poor.

You are not deserting the poor in their misery when you refuse to allow your mind to be filled with pictures of that misery. Poverty can be done away with, not by increasing the number of well to do people who think about poverty, but by increasing the number of poor people who purpose with faith to get rich. The poor do not need charity; they need inspiration. Charity only sends them a loaf of bread to keep them alive in their wretchedness, or gives them an entertainment to make them forget for an hour or two; but inspiration will cause them to rise out of their misery. If you want to help the poor, demonstrate to them that they can become rich; prove it by getting rich yourself.

The only way in which poverty will ever be banished from this world is by getting a large and constantly increasing number of people to practice the teachings of this book. People must be taught to become rich by creation, not by competition. Every man who becomes rich by competition throws down behind him the ladder by which he rises, and keeps others down; but every man who gets rich by creation opens a way for thousands to follow him, and inspires them to do so.

You are not showing hardness of heart or an unfeeling disposition when you refuse to pity poverty, see poverty, read about poverty, or think or talk about it, or to listen to those who do talk about it. Use your will power to keep your mind OFF the subject of poverty, and to keep it fixed with faith and purpose ON the vision of what you want.

CHAPTER 10

Further Use of the Will

YOU cannot retain a true and clear vision of wealth if you are constantly turning your attention to opposing pictures, whether they be external or imaginary.

Do not tell of your past troubles of a financial nature, if you have had them, do not think of them at all. Do no tell of the poverty of your parents, or the hardships of your early life; to do any of these things is to mentally class yourself with the poor for the time being, and it will certainly check the movement of things in your direction.

Put poverty and all things that pertain to poverty completely behind you. You have accepted a certain theory of the universe as being correct, and are resting all your hopes of happiness on its being correct; and what can you gain by giving heed to conflicting theories? Do not read religious books which tell you that the world is soon coming to an end; and do not read the writing of muck-rakers and pessimistic philosophers who tell you that it is going to the devil.

The world is not going to the devil; it is going to God. It is wonderful Becoming.

True, there may be a good many things in existing conditions which are disagreeable; but what is the use of studying them when they are certainly passing away, and when the study of them only tends to check their passing and keep them with us? Why give time and attention to things which are being removed by evolutionary growth, when you can hasten their removal only by promoting the evolutionary growth as far as your part of it goes? No matter how horrible in seeming may be the conditions in certain countries, sections, or places, you waste your time and destroy your own chances by considering them.

You should interest yourself in the world's becoming rich. Think of the riches the world is coming into, instead of the poverty it is growing out of; and bear in mind that the only way in which you can assist the world in growing rich is by growing rich yourself through the creative method--not the competitive one. Give your attention wholly to riches; ignore poverty. Whenever you think or speak of those who are poor, think and speak of them as those who are becoming rich;as those who are to be congratulated rather than pitied. Then they and others will catch the inspiration, and begin to search for the way out.
Because I say that you are to give your whole time and mind and thought to riches, it does not follow that you are to be sordid or mean. To become really rich is the noblest aim you can have in life, for it includes everything else.

On the competitive plane, the struggle to get rich is a Godless scramble for power over other men; but when we come into the creative mind, all this is changed. All that is possible in the way of greatness and soul unfoldment, of service and lofty endeavor, comes by way of getting rich; all is made possible by the use of things. If you lack for physical health, you will find that the attainment of it is conditional on your getting rich. Only those who are emancipated from financial worry, and who have the means to live a care-free existence and follow hygienic practices, can have and retain health.

Moral and spiritual greatness is possible only to those who are above the competitive battle for existence; and only those who are becoming rich on the plane of creative thought are free from the degrading influences of competition. If your heart is set on domestic happiness, remember that love flourishes best where there is refinement, a high level of thought, and freedom from corrupting influences; and these are to be found only where riches are attained by the exercise of creative thought, without strife or rivalry. You can aim at nothing so great or noble, I repeat, as to become rich; and you must fix your attention upon your mental picture of riches, to the exclusion of all that may tend to dim or obscure the vision.

You must learn to see the underlying TRUTH in all things; you must see beneath all seemingly wrong conditions the Great One Life ever moving forward toward fuller expression and more complete happiness. It is the truth that there is no such thing as poverty; that there is only wealth. Some people remain in poverty because they are ignorant of the fact that there is wealth for them; and these can best be taught by showing them the way to affluence in your own person and practice.

Others are poor because, while they feel that there is a way out, they are too intellectually indolent to put forth the mental effort necessary to find that way And by travel it; and for these the very best thing you can do is to arouse their desire by showing them the happiness that comes from being rightly rich. Others still are poor because, while they have some notion of science, they have become so swamped and lost in the maze of metaphysical and occult theories that they do not know which road to take. They try a mixture of many systems and fail in all. For these, again, the very best thing, to do is to show the right way in your own person and practice; an ounce of doing things is worth a pound of theorizing. The very best thing you can do for the whole world is to make the most of yourself. You can serve God and man in no more effective way than by getting rich; that is, if you get rich by the creative method and not by the competetive one.

Another thing. We assert that this book gives in detail the principles of the science of getting rich; and if that is true, you do not need to read any other book upon the subject. This may sound narrow and egotistical, but consider: there is no more scientific method of computation in mathematics than by addition, subtraction, multiplication, and division; no other method is possible. There can be but one shortest distance between two points. There is only one way to think scientifically, and that is to think in the way that leads by the most direct and simple route to the goal. No man has yet formulated a briefer or less complex "system" than the one set forth herein; it has been stripped of all nonessential.

When you commence on this, lay all others aside; put them out of your mind altogether. Read this book every day; keep it with you; commit it to memory, and do not think about other "systems" and theories. If you do, you will begin to have doubts, and to be uncertain and wavering in your thought; and then you will begin to make failures.

After you have made good and become rich, you may study other systems as much as you please; but until you are quite sure that you have gained what you want, do not read anything on this line but this book, unless it be the authors mentioned in the Preface. And read only the most optimistic comments on the world's news; those in Harmony with your picture.

Also, postpone your investigations into the occult. Do not dabble in theosophy, Spiritualism, or kindred studies. It is very likely that the dead still live, and are near; but if they are, let them alone; mind your own business. Wherever the spirits of the dead may be, they have their own work to do, and their own problems to solve; and we have no right to interfere with them. We cannot help them, and it is very doubtful whether they can help us, or whether we have any right to trespass upon their time if they can. Let the dead and the hereafter alone, and solve your own problem; get rich. If you begin to mix with the occult, you will start mental cross currents which will surely bring your hopes to shipwreck.

Now, this and the preceding chapters have brought us to the following statement of basic facts:
There is a thinking stuff from which all things are made, and which, in its original state, permeates, penetrates, and fills the interspaces of the universe. A thought, in this substance, produces the thing that is imaged by the thought. Man can form things in his thought, and, by impressing his thought upon formless substance, can cause the thing he thinks about to be created.

In order to do this, man must pass from the competitive to the creative mind; he must form a clear mental picture of the things he wants, and hold this picture in his thoughts with the fixed PURPOSE to get what he wants, and the unwavering FAITH that he does get what he wants, closing his mind against all that may tend to shake his purpose, dim his vision, or quench his faith. And in addition to all this, we shall now see that he must live and act in a Certain Way.

CHAPTER 11

Acting in the Certain Way

THOUGHT is the creative power, or the impelling force which causes the creative power to act; thinking in a Certain Way will bring riches to you, but you must not rely upon thought alone, paying no attention to personal action. That is the rock upon which many otherwise scientific metaphysical thinkers meet shipwreck--the failure to connect thought with personal action.

We have not yet reached the stage of development, even supposing such a stage to be possible, in which man can create directly from Formless Substance without nature's processes or the work of human hands; man must not only think, but his personal action must supplement his thought. By thought you can cause the gold in the hearts of the mountains to be impelled toward you; but it will not mine itself, refine itself, coin itself into double eagles, and come rolling along the roads seeking its way into your pocket.

Under the impelling power of the Supreme Spirit, men's affairs will be so ordered that some one will be led to mine the gold for you; other men's business transactions will be so directed that the gold will be brought toward you, and you must so arrange your own business affairs that you may be able to receive it when it comes to you. Your thought makes all things, animate and inanimate, work to bring you what you want; but your personal activity must be such that you can rightly receive what you want when it reaches you. You are not to take it as charity, nor to steal it; you must give every man more in use value than he gives you in cash value.

The scientific use of thought consists in forming a clear and distinct mental image of what you want; in holding fast to the purpose to get what you want; and in realizing with grateful faith that you do get what you want. Do not try to 'project' your thought in any mysterious or occult way, with the idea of having it go out and do things for you; that is wasted effort, and will weaken your power to think with sanity.

The action of thought in getting rich is fully explained in the preceding chapters; your faith and purpose positively impress your vision upon Formless Substance, which has THE SAME DESIRE FOR MORE LIFE THAT YOU HAVE; and this vision, received from you, sets all the creative forces at work IN AND THROUGH THEIR REGULAR CHANNELS OF ACTION, but directed toward you.

It is not your part to guide or supervise the creative process; all you have to do with that is to retain your vision, stick to your purpose, and maintain your faith and gratitude.

But you must act in a Certain Way, so that you can appropriate what is yours when it comes to you; so that you can meet the things you have in your picture, and put them in their proper places as they arrive. You can really see the truth of this. When things reach you, they will be in the hands of other men, who will ask an equivalent for them. And you can only get what is yours by giving the other man what is his. Your pocketbook is not going to be transformed into a Fortunata's purse, which shall be always full of money without effort on your part.

This is the crucial point in the science of getting rich; right here, where thought and personal action must be combined. There are very many people who, consciously or unconsciously, set the creative forces in action by the strength and persistence of their desires, but who remain poor because they do not provide for the reception of the thing they want when it comes. By thought, the thing you want is brought to you; by action you receive it. Whatever your action is to be, it is evident that you must act NOW. You cannot act in the past, and it is essential to the clearness of your mental vision that you dismiss the past from your mind. You cannot act in the future, for the future is not here yet. And you cannot tell how you will want to act in any future contingency until that contingency has arrived.

Because you are not in the right business, or the right environment now, do not think that you must postpone action until you get into the right business or environment. And do not spend time in the present taking thought as to the best course in possible future emergencies; have faith in your ability to meet any emergency when it arrives. If you act in the present with your mind on the future, your present action will be with a divided mind, and will not be effective. Put your whole mind into present action.

Do not give your creative impulse to Original Substance, and then sit down and wait for results; if you do, you will never get them. Act now. There is never any time but now, and there never will be any time but now. If you are ever to begin to make ready for the reception of what you want, you must begin now. And your action, whatever it is, must most likely be in your present business or employment, and must be upon the persons and things in your present environment.

You cannot act where you are not; you cannot act where you have been, and you cannot act where you are going to be; you can act only where you are. Do not bother as to whether yesterday's work was well done or ill done; do today's work well. Do not try to do tomorrow's work now; there will be plenty of time to do that when you get to it. Do not try, by occult or mystical means, to act on people or things that are out of your reach. Do not wait for a change of environment, before you act; get a change of environment by action. You can so act upon the environment in which you are now, as to cause yourself to be transferred to a better environment. Hold with faith and purpose the vision of yourself in the better environment, but act upon your present environment with all your heart, and with all your strength, and with all your mind.

Do not spend any time in day dreaming or castle building; hold to the one vision of what you want, and act NOW. Do not cast about seeking some new thing to do, or some strange, unusual, or remarkable action to perform as a first step toward getting rich. It is probable that your actions, at least for some time to come, will be those you have been performing for some time past; but you are to begin now to perform these actions in the Certain Way, which will surely make you rich.

If you are engaged in some business, and feel that it is not the right one for you, do not wait until you get into the right business before you begin to act. Do not feel discouraged, or sit down and lament because you are misplaced. No man was ever so misplaced but that he could not find the right place, and no man ever became so involved in the wrong business but that he could get into the right business. Hold the vision of yourself in the right business, with the purpose to get into it, and the faith that you will get into it, and are getting into it; but ACT in your present business. Use your present business as the means of getting a better one, and use your present enviornment as the means of getting into a better one. Your vision of the right business, if held with faith and purpose, will cause the Supreme to move the right business toward you; and your action, if performed in the Certain Way, will cause you to move toward the business.

If you are an employee, or wage earner, and feel that you must change places in order to get what you want, do not 'project" your thought into space and rely upon it to get you another job. It will probably fail to do so. Hold the vision of yourself in the job you want, while you ACT with faith and purpose on the job you have, and you will certainly get the job you want. Your vision and faith will set the creative force in motion to bring it toward you, and your action will cause the forces in your own environment to move you toward the place you want.

In closing this chapter, we will add another statement to our syllabus: There is a thinking stuff from which all things are made, and which, in its original state, permeates, penetrates, and fills the interspaces of the universe.

A thought, in this substance, produces the thing that is imaged by the thought. Man can form things in his thought, and, by impressing his thought upon formless substance, can cause the thing he thinks about to be created. In order to do this, man must pass from the competitive to the creative mind; he must form a clear mental picture of the things he wants, and hold this picture in his thoughts with the fixed PURPOSE to get what he wants, and the unwavering FAITH that he does get what he wants, closing his mind to all that may tend to shake his purpose, dim his vision, or quench his faith. That he may receive what he wants when it comes, man must act NOW upon the people and things in his present environment.

CHAPTER 12

Efficient Action

You must use your thought as directed in previous chapters, and begin to do what you can do where you are; and you must do ALL that you can do where you are.

You can advance only be being larger than your present place; and no man is larger than his present place who leaves undone any of the work pertaining to that place. The world is advanced only by those who more than fill their present places. If no man quite filled his present place, you can see that there must be a going backward in everything. Those who do not quite fill their present places are dead weight upon society, government, commerce, and industry; they must be carried along by others at a great expense. The progress of the world is retarded only by those who do not fill the places they are holding; they belong to a former age and a lower stage or plane of life, and their tendency is toward degeneration. No society could advance if every man was smaller than his place; social evolution is guided by the law of physical and mental evolution.

In the animal world, evolution is caused by excess of life. When an organism has more life than can be expressed in the functions of its own plane, it develops the organs of a higher plane, and a new species is originated. There never would have been new species had there not been organisms which more than filled their places.

The law is exactly the same for you; your getting rich depends upon your applying this principle to your own affairs. Every day is either a successful day or a day of failure; and it is the successful days which get you what you want. If everyday is a failure, you can never get rich; while if every day is a success, you cannot fail to get rich. If there is something that may be done today, and you do not do it, you have failed in so far as that thing is concerned; and the consequences may be more disastrous than you imagine.

You cannot foresee the results of even the most trivial act; you do not know the workings of all the forces that have been set moving in your behalf. Much may be depending on your doing some simple act; it may be the very thing which is to open the door of opportunity to very great possibilities. You can never know all the combinations which Supreme Intelligence is making for you in the world of things and of things and of human affairs; your neglect or failure to do some small thing may cause a long delay in getting what you want.
Do, every day, ALL that can be done that day.

There is, however, a limitation or qualification of the above that you must take into account. You are not to overwork, nor to rush blindly into your business in the effort to do the greatest possible number of things in the shortest possible time. You are not to try to do tomorrow's work today, nor to do a week's work in a day. It is really not he number of things you do, but the EFFICIENCY of each separate action that counts.

Every act is, in itself, either a success or a failure.

Every act is, in itself, either effective or inefficient.

Every inefficient act is a failure, and if you spend your life in doing inefficient acts, your whole life will be a failure.

The more things you do, the worse for you, if all your acts are inefficient ones. On the other hand, every efficient act is a success in itself, and if every act of your life is an efficient one, your whole life MUST be a success.

The cause of failure is doing too many things in an inefficient manner, and not doing enough things in an efficient manner. You will see that it is a self-evident proposition that if you do not do any inefficient acts, and if you do a sufficient number of efficient acts, you will become rich. If, now, it is possible for you to make each act an efficient one, you see again that the getting of riches is reduced to an exact science, like mathematics.

The matter turns, then, on the questions whether you can make each separate act a success in itself. And this you can certainly do. You can make each act a success, because ALL Power is working with you; and ALL Power cannot fail. Power is at your service; and to make each act efficient you have only to put power into it.

Every action is either strong or weak; and when every one is strong, you are acting in the Certain Way which will make you rich. Every act can be made strong and efficient by holding your vision while you are doing it, and putting the whole power of your FAITH and PURPOSE into it.

It is at this point that the people fail who separate mental power from personal action. They use the power of mind in one place and at one time, and they act in another pace and at another time. So their acts are not successful in themselves; too many of them are inefficient. But if ALL Power goes into every act, no matter how commonplace, every act will be a success in itself; and as in the nature of things every success opens the way to other successes, your progress toward what you want, and the progress of what you want toward you, will become increasingly rapid.

Remember that successful action is cumulative in its results. Since the desire for more life is inherent in all things, when a man begins to move toward larger life more things attach themselves to him, and the influence of his desire is multiplied. Do, every day, all that you can do that day, and do each act in an efficient manner.

In saying that you must hold your vision while you are doing each act, however trivial or commonplace, I do not mean to say that it is necessary at all times to see the vision distinctly to its smallest details. It should be the work of your leisure hours to use your imagination on the details of your vision, and to contemplate them until they are firmly fixed upon memory. If you wish speedy results, spend practically all your spare time in this practice. By continuous contemplation you will get the picture of what you want, even to the smallest details, so firmly fixed upon your mind, and so completely transferred to the mind of Formless Substance, that in your working hours you need only to mentally refer to the picture to stimulate your faith and purpose, and cause your best effort to be put forth.

Contemplate your picture in your leisure hours until your consciousness is so full of it that you can grasp it instantly. You will become so enthused with its bright promises that the mere thought of it will call forth the strongest energies of your whole being.

Let us again repeat our syllabus, and by slightly changing the closing statements bring it to the point we have now reached.

There is a thinking stuff from which all things are made, and which, in its original state, permeates, penetrates, and fills the interspaces of the universe. A thought, in this substance, produces the thing that is imaged by the thought. Man can form things in his thought, and, by impressing his thought upon formless substance, can cause the thing he thinks about to be created. In order to do this, man must pass from the competitive to the creative mind; he must form a clear mental picture of the things he wants, and do, with faith and purpose, all that can be done each day, doing each separate thing in an efficient manner.

CHAPTER 13

Getting into the Right Business

SUCCESS, in any particular business, depends for one thing upon your possessing in a well-developed state the faculties required in that business. Without good musical faculty no one can succeed as a teacher of music; without well-developed mechanical faculties no one can achieve great success in any of the mechanical trades; without tact and the commercial faculties no one can succeed in mercantile pursuits. But to possess in a well-developed state the faculties required in your particular vocation does not insure getting rich. There are musicians who have remarkable talent, and who yet remain poor; there are blacksmiths, carpenters, and so on who have excellent mechanical ability, but who do not get rich; and there are merchants with good faculties for dealing with men who nevertheless fail.

The different faculties are tools; it is essential to have good tools, but it is also essential that the tools should be used in the Right Way. One man can take a sharp saw, a square, a good plane, and so on, and build a handsome article of furniture; another man can take the same tools and set to work to duplicate the article, but his production will be a botch. He does not know how to use good tools in a successful way.

The various faculties of your mind are the tools with which you must do the work which is to make you rich; it will be easier for you to succeed if you get into a business for which you are well equipped with mental tools. Generally speaking, you will do best in that business which will use your strongest faculties; the one for which you are naturally "best fitted." But there are limitations to this statement, also. No man should regard his vocation as being irrevocably fixed by the tendencies with which he was born.

You can get rich in ANY business, for if you have not the right talent for you can develop that talent; it merely means that you will have to make your tools as you go along, instead of confining yourself to the use of those with which you were born. It will be EASIER for you to succeed in a vocation for which you already have the talents in a well-developed state; but you CAN succeed in any vocation, for you can develop any rudimentary talent, and there is no talent of which you have not at least the rudiment.

You will get rich most easily in point of effort, if you do that for which you are best fitted; but you will get rich most satisfactorily if you do that which you WANT to do.

Doing what you want to do is life; and there is no real satisfaction in living if we are compelled to be forever doing something which we do not like to do, and can never do what we want to do. And it is certain that you can do what you want to do; the desire to do it is proof that you have within you the power which can do it.

Desire is a manifestation of power. The desire to play music is the power which can play music seeking expression and development; the desire to invent mechanical devices is the mechanical talent seeking expression and development. Where there is no power, either developed or undeveloped, to do a thing, there is never any desire to do that thing; and where there is strong desire to do a thing, it is certain proof that the power to do it is strong, and only requires to be developed and applied in the Right Way.

All things else being equal, it is best to select the business for which you have the best developed talent; but if you have a strong desire to engage in any particular line of work, you should select that work as the ultimate end at which you aim. You can do what you want to do, and it is your right and privilege to follow the business or a vocation which will be most congenial and pleasant. You are not obliged to do what you do not like to do, and should not do it except as a means to bring you to the doing of the thing you want to do.

If there are past mistakes whose consequences have placed you in an undesirable business or environment, you may be obliged for some time to do what you do not like to do; but you can make the doing of it pleasant by knowing that it is making it possible for you to come to the doing of what you want to do. If you feel that you are not in the right vocation, do not act too hastily in trying to get into another one. The best way, generally, to change business or environment is by growth. Do not be afraid to make a sudden and radical change if the opportunity is presented, and you feel after careful consideration that it is the right opportunity; but never take sudden or radical action when you are in doubt as to the wisdom of doing so. There is never any hurry on the creative plane; and there is no lack of opportunity.

When you get out of the competitive mind you will understand that you never need to act hastily. No one else is going to beat you to the thing you want to do; there is enough for all. If one space is taken, another and a better one will be opened for you a little farther on; there is plenty of time. When you are in doubt, wait. Fall back on the contemplation of your vision, and increase your faith and purpose; and by all means, in times of doubt and indecision, cultivate gratitude.
A day or two spent in contemplating the vision of what you want, and in earnest thanksgiving that you are getting it, will bring your mind into such close relationship with the Supreme that you will make no mistake when you do act. There is a mind which knows all there is to know; and you can come into close unity with this mind by faith and the purpose to advance in life, if you have deep gratitude.

Mistakes come from acting hastily, or from acting in fear or doubt, or in forgetfulness of the Right Motive, which is more life to all, and less to none. As you go on in the Certain Way, opportunities will come to you in increasing number; and you will need to be very steady in your faith and purpose, and to keep in close touch with the All Mind by reverent gratitude. Do all that you can do in a perfect manner every day, but do it without haste, worry, or fear. Go as fast as you can, but never hurry.

Remember that in the moment you begin to hurry you cease to be a creator and become a competitor; you drop back upon the old plane again. Whenever you find yourself hurrying, call a halt; fix your attention on the mental image of the thing you want, and begin to give thanks that you are getting it. The exercise of GRATITUDE will never fail to strengthen your faith and renew your purpose.

CHAPTER 14

The Impression of Increase

WHETHER you change your vocation or not, your actions for the present must be those pertaining to the business in which you are now engaged. You can get into the business you want by making constructive use of the business you are already established in; by doing your daily work in a Certain Way.

And in so far as your business consists in dealing with other men, whether personally or by letter, the key-thought of all your efforts must be to convey to their minds the impression of increase. Increase is what all men and all women are seeking; it is the urge of the Formless Intelligence within them, seeking fuller expression.

The desire for increase is inherent in all nature; it is the fundamental impulse of the universe. All human activities are based on the desire for increase; people are seeking more food, more clothes, better shelter, more luxury, more beauty, more knowledge, more pleasure-- increase in something, more life. Every living thing is under this necessity for continuous advancement; where increase of life ceases, dissolution and death set in at once. Man instinctively knows this, and hence he is forever seeking more. The normal desire for increased wealth is not an evil or a reprehensible thing; it is simply the desire for more abundant life; it is aspiration. And because it is the deepest instinct of their natures, all men and women are attracted to him who can give them more of the means of life.

In following the Certain Way as described in the foregoing pages, you are getting continuous increase for yourself, and you are giving it to all with whom you deal. You are a creative center, from which increase is given off to all. Be sure of this, and convey assurance of the fact to every man, woman, and child with whom you come in contact. No matter how small the transaction, even if it be only the selling of a stick of candy to a little child, put into it the thought of increase, and make sure that the customer is impressed with the thought.

Convey the impression of advancement with everything you do, so that all people shall receive the impression that you are an Advancing Man, and that you advance all who deal with you. Even to the people whom you meet in a social way, without any thought of business, and to whom you do not try to sell anything, give the thought of increase. You can convey this impression by holding the unshakable faith that you, yourself, are in the Way of Increase; and by letting this faith inspire, fill, and permeate every action.

Do everything that you do in the firm conviction that you are an advancing personality, and that you are giving advancement to everybody. Feel that you are getting rich, and that in so doing you are making others rich, and conferring benefits on all.

Do not boast or brag of your success, or talk about it unnecessarily; true faith is never boastful. Wherever you find a boastful person, you find one who is secretly doubtful and afraid. Simply feel the faith, and let it work out in every transaction; let every act and tone and look express the quiet assurance that you are getting rich; that you are already rich. Words will not be necessary to communicate this feeling to others; they will feel the sense of increase when in your presence, and will be attracted to you again.

You must so impress others that they will feel that in associating with you they will get increase for themselves. See that you give them a use value greater than the cash value you are taking from them. Take an honest pride in doing this, and let everybody know it; and you will have no lack of customers. People will go where they are given increase; and the Supreme, which desires increase in all, and which knows all, will move toward you men and women who have never heard of you. Your business will increase rapidly, and you will be surprised at the unexpected benefits which will come to you. You will be able from day to day to make larger combinations, secure greater advantages, and to go on into a more congenial vocation if you desire to do so.

But doing thing all this, you must never lose sight of your vision of what you want, or your faith and purpose to get what you want. Let me here give you another word of caution in regard to motives. Beware of the insidious temptation to seek for power over other men. Nothing is so pleasant to the unformed or partially developed mind as the exercise of power or dominion over others. The desire to rule for selfish gratification has been the curse of the world. For countless ages kings and lords have drenched the earth with blood in their battles to extend their dominions; this not to seek more life for all, but to get more power for themselves.

Today, the main motive in the business and industrial world is the same; men Marshal their armies of dollars, and lay waste the lives and hearts of millions in the same mad scramble for power over others. Commercial kings, like political kings, are inspired by the lust for power. Look out for the temptation to seek for authority, to become a "master," to be considered as one who is above the common herd, to impress others by lavish display, and so on. The mind that seeks for mastery over others is the competitive mind; and the competitive mind is not the creative one. In order to master your environment and your destiny, it is not at all necessary that you should rule over your fellow men and indeed, when you fall into the world's struggle for the high places, you begin to be conquered by fate and environment, and your getting rich becomes a matter of chance and speculation.

Beware of the competitive mind!! No better statement of the principle of creative action can be formulated than the favorite declaration of the late "Golden Rule" Jones of Toledo: "What I want for myself, I want for everybody."

CHAPTER 15

The Advancing Man

WHAT I have said in the last chapter applies as well to the professional man and the wage-earner as to the man who is engaged in mercantile business. No matter whether you are a physician, a teacher, or a clergyman, if you can give increase of life to others and make them sensible of the fact, they will be attracted to you, and you will get rich. The physician who holds the vision of himself as a great and successful healer, and who works toward the complete realization of that vision with faith and purpose, as described in former chapters, will come into such close touch with the Source of Life that he will be phenomenally successful; patients will come to him in throngs.

No one has a greater opportunity to carry into effect the teaching of this book than the practitioner of medicine; it does not matter to which of the various schools he may belong, for the principle of healing is common to all of them, and may be reached by all alike. The Advancing Man in medicine, who holds to a clear mental image of himself as successful, and who obeys the laws of faith, purpose, and gratitude, will cure every curable case he undertakes, no matter what remedies he may use. In the field of religion, the world cries out for the clergyman who can teach his hearers the true science of abundant life. He who masters the details of the science of getting rich, together with the allied sciences of being well, of being great, and of winning love, and who teaches these details from the pulpit, will never lack for a congregation. This is the gospel that the world needs; it will give increase of life, and men will hear it gladly, and will give liberal support to the man who brings it to them.

What is now needed is a demonstration of the science of life from the pulpit. We want preachers who can not only tell us how, but who in their own persons will show us how. We need the preacher who will himself be rich, healthy, great, and beloved, to teach us how to attain to these things; and when he comes he will find a numerous and loyal following. The same is true of the teacher who can inspire the children with the faith and purpose of the advancing life. He will never be "out of a job." And any teacher who has this faith and purpose can give it to his pupils; he cannot help giving it to them if it is part of his own life and practice.

What is true of the teacher, preacher, and physician is true of the lawyer, dentist, real estate man, insurance agent--of everybody. The combined mental and personal action I have described is infallible; it cannot fail. Every man and woman who follows these instructions steadily, perseveringly, and to the letter, will get rich. The law of the Increase of Life is as mathematically certain in its operation as the law of gravitation; getting rich is an exact science.

The wage earner will find this as true of his case as of any of the others mentioned. Do not feel that you have no chance to get rich because you are working where there is no visible opportunity for advancement, where wages are small and the cost of living high. Form your clear mental vision of what you want, and begin to act with faith and purpose.

Do all the work you can do, every day, and do each piece of work in a perfectly successful manner; put the power of success, and the purpose to get rich, into everything that you do. But do not do this merely with the idea of currying favor with your employer, in the hope that he, or those above you, will see your good work and advance you; it is not likely that they will do so. The man who is merely a "good" workman, filling his place to the very best of his ability, and satisfied with that, is valuable to his employer; and it is not to the employer's interest to promote him; he is worth more where he is.

To secure advancement, something more is necessary than to be too large for your place. The man who is certain to advance is the one who is too big for his place, and who has a clear concept of what he wants to be; who knows that he can become what he wants to be and who is determined to BE what he wants to be. Do not try to more than fill your present place with a view to pleasing your employer; do it with the idea of advancing yourself. Hold the faith and purpose of increase during work hours, after work hours, and before work hours. Hold it in such a way that every person who comes in contact with you, whether foreman, fellow workman, or social acquaintance, will feel the power of purpose radiating from you; so that every one will get the sense of advancement and increase from you. Men will be attracted to you, and if there is no possibility for advancement in your present job, you will very soon see an opportunity to take another job.

There is a Power which never fails to present opportunity to the Advancing Man who is moving in obedience to law. God cannot help helping you, if you act in a Certain Way; He must do so in order to help Himself. There is nothing in your circumstances or in the industrial situation that can keep you down. If you cannot get rich working for the steel trust, you can get rich on a ten-acre farm; and if you begin to move in the Certain Way, you will certainly escape from the "clutches" of the steel trust and get on to the farm or wherever else you wish to be.

If a few thousands of its employees would enter upon the Certain Way, the steel trust would soon be in a bad plight; it would have to give its workingmen more opportunity, or go out of business. Nobody has to work for a trust; the trusts can keep men in so called hopeless conditions only so long as there are men who are too ignorant to know of the science of getting rich, or too intellectually slothful to practice it.

Begin this way of thinking and acting, and your faith and purpose will make you quick to see any opportunity to better your condition. Such opportunities will speedily come, for the Supreme, working in All, and working for you, will bring them before you. Do not wait for an opportunity to be all that you want to be; when an opportunity to be more than you are now is presented and you feel impelled toward it, take it. It will be the first step toward a greater opportunity. There is no

47

such thing possible in this universe as a lack of opportunities for the man who is living the advancing life.

It is inherent in the constitution of the cosmos that all things shall be for him and work together for his good; and he must certainly get rich if he acts and thinks in the Certain Way. So let wage-earning men and women study this book with great care, and enter with confidence upon the course of action it prescribes; it will not fail.

CHAPTER 16

Some Cautions, and Concluding Observations

MANY people will scoff at the idea that there is an exact science of getting rich; holding the impression that the supply of wealth is limited, they will insist that social and governmental institutions must be changed before even any considerable number of people can acquire a competence.

But this is not true.

It is true that existing governments keep the masses in poverty, but this is because the masses do not think and act in the Certain Way. If the masses begin to move forward as suggested in this book, neither governments nor industrial systems can check them; all systems must be modified to accommodate the forward movement. If the people have the Advancing Mind, have the Faith that they can become rich, and move forward with the fixed purpose to become rich, nothing can possibly keep them in poverty.

Individuals may enter upon the Certain Way at any time, and under any government, and make themselves rich; and when any considerable number of individuals do so under any government, they will cause the system to be so modified as to open the way for others. The more men who get rich on the competitive plane, the worse for others; the more who get rich on the creative plane, the better for others. The economic salvation of the masses can only be accomplished by getting a large number of people to practice the scientific method set down in this book, and become rich. These will show others the way, and inspire them with a desire for real life, with the faith that it can be attained, and with the purpose to attain it.

For the present, however, it is enough to know that neither the government under which you live nor the capitalistic or competitive system of industry can keep you from getting rich. When you enter upon the creative plane of thought you will rise above all these things and become a citizen of another kingdom. But remember that your thought must be held upon the creative plane; you are never for an instant to be betrayed into regarding the supply as limited, or into acting on the moral level of competition.

Whenever you do fall into old ways of thought, correct yourself instantly; for when you are in the competitive mind, you have lost the cooperation of the Mind of the Whole. Do not spend any time in planning as to how you will meet possible emergencies in the future, except as the necessary policies may affect your actions today. You are concerned with doing today's work in a perfectly successful manner, and not with emergencies which may arise tomorrow; you can attend to them as they come.

Do not concern yourself with questions as to how you shall surmount obstacles which may loom upon your business horizon, unless you can see plainly that your course must be altered today in order to avoid them. No matter how tremendous an obstruction may appear at a distance, you will find that if you go on in the Certain Way it will disappear as you approach it, or that a way over, though, or around it will appear. No possible combination of circumstances can defeat a man or woman who is proceeding to get rich along strictly scientific lines. No man or woman who obeys the law can fail to get rich, any more than one can multiply two by two and fail to get four.

Give no anxious thought to possible disasters, obstacles, panics, or unfavorable combinations of circumstances; it is time enough to meet such things when they present themselves before you in the immediate present, and you will find that every difficulty carries with it the wherewithal for its overcoming.

Guard your speech. Never speak of yourself, your affairs, or of anything else in a discouraged or discouraging way. Never admit the possibility of failure, or speak in a way that infers failure as a possibility. Never speak of the times as being hard, or of business conditions as being doubtful. Times may be hard and business doubtful for those who are on the competitive plane, but they can never be so for you; you can create what you want, and you are above fear. When others are having hard times and poor business, you will find your greatest opportunities.

Train yourself to think of and to look upon the world as a something which is Becoming, which is growing; and to regard seeming evil as being only that which is undeveloped. Always speak in terms of advancement; to do otherwise is to deny your faith, and to deny your faith is to lose it. Never allow yourself to feel disappointed. You may expect to have a certain thing at a certain time, and not get it at that time; and this will appear to you like failure. But if you hold to your faith you will find that the failure is only apparent. Go on in the certain way, and if you do not receive that thing, you will receive something so much better that you will see that the seeming failure was really a great success.

A student of this science had set his mind on making a certain business combination which seemed to him at the time to be very desirable, and he worked for some, weeks to bring it about. When the crucial time came, the thing failed in a perfectly inexplicable way; it was as if some unseen influence had been working secretly against him. He was not disappointed; on the contrary, he thanked God that his desire had been overruled, and went steadily on with a grateful mind. In a few weeks an opportunity so much better came his way that he would not have made the first deal on any account; and he saw that a Mind which knew more than he knew had prevented him from losing the greater good by entangling himself with the lesser.

That is the way every seeming failure will work out for you, if you keep your faith, hold to your purpose, have gratitude, and do, every day all that can be done that day, doing each separate act in a successful manner. When you make a failure, it is because you have not asked for enough; keep on, and a larger thing then you were seeking will certainly come to you. Remember this.

You will not fail because you lack the necessary talent to do what you wish to do. If you go on as I have directed, you will develop all the talent that is necessary to the doing of your work. It is not within the scope of this book to deal with the science of cultivating talent; but it is as certain and simple as the process of getting rich. However, do not hesitate or waver for fear that when you come to any certain place you will fail for lack of ability; keep right on, and when you come to that place, the ability will be furnished to you. The same source of Ability which enabled the untaught Lincoln to do the greatest work in government ever accomplished by a single man is open to you; you may draw upon all the mind there is for wisdom to use in meeting the responsibilities which are laid upon you.

Go on in full faith. Study this book. Make it your constant companion until you have mastered all the ideas contained in it. While you are getting firmly established in this faith, you will do well to give up most recreations and pleasure; and to stay away from places where ideas conflicting with these are advanced in lectures or sermons. Do not read pessimistic or conflicting literature, or get into arguments upon the matter. Do very little reading, outside of the writers mentioned in the Preface. Spend most of your leisure time in contemplating your vision, and in cultivating gratitude, and in reading this book. It contains all you need to know of the science of getting rich; and you will find all the essentials summed up in the following chapter.

CHAPTER 17

Summary of the Science of Getting Rich

THERE is a thinking stuff from which all things are made, and which, in its original state, permeates, penetrates, and fills the interspaces of the universe. A thought in this substance produces the thing that is imaged by the thought. Man can form things in his thought, and by impressing his thought upon formless substance can cause the thing he thinks about to be created.

In order to do this, man must pass from the competitive to the creative mind; otherwise he cannot be in harmony with the Formless Intelligence, which is always creative and never competitive in spirit.

Man may come into full harmony with the Formless Substance by entertaining a lively and sincere gratitude for the blessings it bestows upon him. Gratitude unifies the mind of man with the intelligence of Substance, so that man's thoughts are received by the Formless. Man can remain upon the creative plane only by uniting himself with the Formless Intelligence through a deep and continuous feeling of gratitude.

Man must form a clear and definite mental image of the things he wishes to have, to do, or to become; and he must hold this mental image in his thoughts, while being deeply grateful to the Supreme that all his desires are granted to him. The man who wishes to get rich must spend his leisure hours in contemplating his Vision, and in earnest thanksgiving that the reality is being given to him. Too much stress cannot be laid on the importance of frequent contemplation of the mental image, coupled with unwavering faith and devout gratitude. This is the process by which the impression is given to the Formless, and the creative forces set in motion.

The creative energy works through the established channels of natural growth, and of the industrial and social order. All that is included in his mental image will surely be brought to the man who follows the instructions given above, and whose faith does not waver. What he wants will come to him through the ways of established trade and commerce.

In order to receive his own when it shall come to him, man must be active; and this activity can only consist in more than filling his present place. He must keep in mind the Purpose to get rich through the realization of his mental image. And he must do, every day all that can be done that day taking care to do each act in a successful manner. He must give to every man a use value in excess of the cash value he receives, so that each transaction makes for more life; and he must so hold the Advancing Thought that the impression of increase will be communicated to all with whom he comes in contact. The men and women who practice the foregoing instructions will certainly get rich; and the riches they receive will be in exact proportion to the definiteness of their vision, the fixity of their purpose, the steadiness of their faith, and the depth of their gratitude.

THE END

The Science of Being Great

by Wallace Wattles

Table of Contents

The Science of Being Great
Chapter 1
Any Person May Become Great

THERE is a Principle of Power in every person. By the intelligent use and direction of this principle, man can develop his own mental faculties. Man has an inherent power by which he may grow in whatever direction he pleases. There does not appear to be any limit to the possibilities of his growth. No man has yet become so great in any faculty so it is possible for someone else to become greater. The possibility is in the Original Substance from which man is made. Genius is Omniscience flowing into man. Genius is more than talent. Talent may merely be one faculty developed out of proportion to other faculties, but genius is the union of man and God in the acts of the soul. Great men are always greater than their deeds. They are in connection with a reserve power that is without limit. We do not know where the boundary of the mental powers of man is; we do not even know that there is a boundary. The power of conscious growth is not given to the lower animals; it is man's alone and may be developed and increased by him. The lower animals can, to a great extent, be trained and developed by man; but man can train and develop himself. He alone has this power, and he has it to an apparently unlimited extent. The purpose of life for man is growth, just as the purpose of life for trees and plants is growth. Trees and plants grow automatically and along fixed lines; man can grow as he will. Trees and plants can only develop certain possibilities and characteristics; man can develop any power which has been shown by any person, anywhere. Nothing that is possible in spirit is impossible in flesh and blood. Nothing that man can think is impossible in action. Nothing that man can imagine is impossible of realization. Man is formed for growth, and he is under the necessity of growing. It is essential to his happiness that he should continuously advance. Life without progress becomes unendurable, and the person who ceases from growth must either become imbecile or insane. The greater and more harmonious and well-rounded his growth, the happier man will be. There is no possibility in any man that is not in every man; but if they proceed naturally, no two men will grow into the same thing, or be alike. Every man comes into the world with a predisposition to grow along certain lines, and growth is easier for him along those lines than in any other way. This is a wise provision, for it gives endless variety. It is as if a gardener should throw all his bulbs into one basket; to the superficial observer they would look alike, but growth reveals a tremendous difference. So of men and women; they are like the basket of bulbs. One may be a rose and add brightness and color to some dark corner of the world; one may be a lily and teach a lesson of love and purity to every eye that sees; one may be a climbing vine and hide the rugged outlines of some dark rock; one may be a great oak among whose boughs the birds shall nest and sing, and beneath whose shade the flocks shall rest at noon, but every one will be something worth while, something rare, something perfect. There are undreamed of possibilities in the common lives all around us. In a large sense, there are no "common" people. In times of national stress and peril the cracker-box loafer of the corner store and the village drunkard become heroes and statesmen through the quickening of the Principle of Power within them. There is a genius in every man and woman, waiting to be brought forth. Every village has its great man or woman; someone to whom all go for advice in time of trouble; someone who is instinctively recognized as being great in wisdom and insight. To such a one the minds of the whole community turn in times of local crisis; he is tacitly recognized as being great. He does small things in a great way. He could do great things as well if he did but undertake them; so can any man; so can you. The Principle of Power gives us just what we ask of it; if we only undertake little things, it only gives us power for little things; but if we try to do great things in a great way it gives us all the power there is. But beware of undertaking great things in a small way; of that we shall speak further on. There are two mental attitudes a man may take. One makes him like a football. It has resilience and reacts strongly when force is applied to it, but it originates nothing; it never acts of itself. There is no power within it. Men of this type are controlled by circumstances and environment; their destinies are decided by things external to themselves. The Principle of Power within them is never really active at all. They never speak or act from within. The other attitude makes man like a flowing spring. Power comes out from the center of him. He has within him a well of water springing up into everlasting life, he radiates force; he is felt by his environment. The Principle of Power in him is in constant action. He is self-active. "He hath life in himself." No greater good can come to any man or woman than to become self-active. All the experiences of life are designed by Providence to force men and women into self-activity; to compel them to cease being creatures of circumstances and master their environment. In his lowest stage, man is the child of chance and circumstance and the slave of fear. His acts are all reactions resulting from the impingement upon him of forces in his environment. He acts only as he is acted upon; he originates nothing. But the lowest savage has within him a Principle of Power sufficient to master all that he fears; and if he learns this and becomes self-active, he becomes as one of the gods. Nothing was ever in any man that is not in you; no man ever had more spiritual or mental power than you can attain, or did greater things than you can accomplish. You can become what you want to be.

The Science of Being Great
Chapter 2
Heredity and Opportunity

YOU are not barred from attaining greatness by heredity. No matter who or what your ancestors may have been or how unlearned or lowly their station, the upward way is open for you. There is no such thing as inheriting a fixed mental position; no matter how small the mental capital we receive from our parents, it may be increased; no man is born incapable of growth. Heredity counts for something. We are born with subconscious mental tendencies; as, for instance, a tendency to melancholy, or cowardice, or to ill-temper; but all these subconscious tendencies may be overcome. When the real man awakens and comes forth he can throw them off very easily. Nothing of this kind need keep you down; if you have inherited undesirable mental tendencies, you can eliminate them and put desirable tendencies in their places. An inherited mental trait is a habit of thought of your father or mother impressed upon your subconscious mind; you can substitute the opposite impression by forming the opposite habit of thought. You can substitute a habit of cheerfulness for a tendency to despondency; you can overcome cowardice or ill temper. Heredity may count for something, too, in an inherited conformation of the skull. There is something in phrenology, if not so much as its exponents claim. It is true that the different faculties are localized in the brain, and that the power of a faculty depends upon the number of active brain cells in its area. A faculty whose brain area is large is likely to act with more power than one whose cranial section is small; hence persons with certain conformations of the skull show talent as musicians, orators, mechanics, and so on. It has been argued from this that a man's cranial formation must, to a great extent, decide his station in life, but this is an error. It has been found that a small brain section, with many fine and active cells, gives as powerful expression to faculty as a larger brain with coarser cells; and it has been found that by turning the Principle of Power into any section of the brain, with the will and purpose to develop a particular talent, the brain cells may be multiplied indefinitely. Any faculty, power, or talent you possess, no matter how small or rudimentary, may be increased; you can multiply the brain cells in this particular area until it acts as powerfully as you wish. It is true that you can act most easily through those faculties that are now most largely developed. You can, with the least effort, do the things which "come naturally." But it is also true that if you will make the necessary effort you can develop any talent. You can do what you desire to do and become what you want to be. When you fix upon some ideal and proceed as herein directed, all the power of your being is turned into the faculties required in the realization of that ideal; more blood and nerve force go to the corresponding sections of the brain, and the cells are quickened, increased, and multiplied in number. The proper use of the mind of man will build a brain capable of doing what the mind wants to do. The brain does not make the man; the man makes the brain. Your place in life is not fixed by heredity. Nor are you condemned to the lower levels by circumstances or lack of opportunity. The Principle of Power in man is sufficient for all the requirements of his soul. No possible combination of circumstances can keep him down, if he makes his personal attitude right and determines to rise. The power which formed man and purposed him for growth also controls the circumstances of society, industry, and government; and this power is never divided against itself. The power which is in you is in the things around you, and when you begin to move forward, the things will arrange themselves for your advantage, as described in later chapters of this book. Man was formed for growth, and all things external were designed to promote his growth. No sooner does a man awaken his soul and enter on the advancing way than he finds that not only is God for him, but nature, society, and his fellow men are for him also; and all things work together for his good if he obeys the law. Poverty is no bar to greatness, for poverty can always be removed. Linnaeus the naturalist, had only forty dollars with which to educate himself; he mended his own shoes and often had to beg meals from his friends. Hugh Miller, apprenticed to a stone mason, began to study geology in a quarry. George Stephenson, inventor of the locomotive engine, and one of the greatest of civil engineers, was a coal miner, working in a mine, when he awakened and began to think. James Watt was a sickly child, and was not strong enough to be sent to school. Abraham Lincoln was a poor boy. In each of these cases we see God as a Principle of Power in the man which lifts him above all opposition and adversity. There is a Principle of Power in you; if you use it and apply it in a certain way you can overcome all heredity, and master all circumstances and conditions and become a great and powerful personality.

The Science of Being Great
Chapter 3
The Source of Power

MAN'S brain, body, mind, faculties, and talents are the mere instruments he uses in demonstrating greatness; in and of themselves they do not make him great. A man may have a large brain and a good mind, strong faculties, and brilliant talents, and yet he is not a great man unless he uses all these in a great way. That quality which enables man to use his abilities in a great way makes him great; and to that quality we give the name of wisdom. Wisdom is the essential basis of greatness. Wisdom is the power to perceive the best ends to aim at and the best means for reaching those ends. It is the power to perceive the right thing to do. The man who is wise enough to know the right thing to do, who is good enough to wish to do only the right thing, and who is able and strong enough to do the right thing is a truly great man. He will instantly become marked as a personality of power in any community and men will delight to do him honor. Wisdom is dependent upon knowledge. Where there is complete ignorance there can be no wisdom, no knowledge of the right thing to do. Man's knowledge is comparatively limited and so his wisdom must be small. Unless he can connect his mind with a knowledge greater than that of his own and draw inspiration from the wisdom that his own limitations otherwise deny him. This he can do; this is what the really great men and women have done. Man's knowledge is limited and uncertain therefore he cannot have wisdom in himself. Only G-d knows all truth. Therefore only God can have real wisdom or know the right thing to do at all times, and man can receive wisdom from God. For example, Abraham Lincoln had limited education but he had the power to perceive truth. In Lincoln we see that real wisdom consisted of knowing the right thing to do at all times and under all circumstances by having the will to do the right thing, having the talent, and the ability to be competent and able to do the right thing. Back in the days of the abolition agitation, and during the compromise period, when all other men were more or less confused as to what was right or as to what ought to be done, Lincoln was never uncertain. He saw through the superficial arguments of the pro-slavery men, the impracticability and fanaticism of the abolitionists, he determined the right ends to aim at, and he saw the best means to attain those ends. It was because men recognized that he perceived truth and knew the right thing to do that they made him president. Any man who develops the power to perceive truth, and who can show that he always knows the right thing to do and that he can be trusted to do the right thing, will be honored and advanced. The whole world is looking eagerly for such men. When Lincoln became president he was surrounded by a multitude of so-called able advisers yet hardly any two of them were in agreement. At times they were all opposed to his policies and at times almost the whole North was opposed to what he proposed to do. But he saw the truth when others were misled by Appearances. His judgment was seldom or ever wrong. He was at once the most able statesman and the best soldier of the period. Where did he, acomparatively unlearned man, get this wisdom? It was not due to some peculiar formation of his skull or to some fineness of texture of his brain. It was not, due to some physical characteristic. It was not even a quality of mind due to superior reasoning power. Knowledge of truth is not often reached by the processes of reason. It was due to a spiritual insight. He perceived truth, but where did he perceive it and whence did the perception come? We see something similar in George Washington, whose faith and courage, due to his perception of truth, held the colonies together during the long and often apparently hopeless struggle of the Revolution. We see something of the same thing in the phenomenal genius of Napoleon, who always knew, in military matters, the best means to adopt. We see that the greatness of Napoleon was in nature rather than in Napoleon. We discover in both Washington and Lincoln something greater than either Of them. And we see the same thing in all great men and women. They perceive truth; but truth cannot be perceived until it exists. And there can be no truth until there is a mind to perceive it. Truth does not exist apart from mind. Wisdom is obtained by understanding what God wants from us.

The Science of Being Great
Chapter 4
The Mind of God

THERE is an Intelligence which is in all things and through all things. This is the one real substance. From it all things proceed. It is Intelligent Substance or Mind Stuff. It is G-d. Where there is no substance there can be no intelligence; for where there is no substance there is nothing. Where there is thought there must be a substance which thinks. Thought cannot be function, for function is motion, and it is inconceivable that mere motion should think. Thought cannot be vibration, for vibration is motion, and that motion should be intelligent is not thinkable. Motion is nothing but the moving of substance; if there be intelligence shown it must be in the substance and not in the motion. Thought cannot be the result of motions in the brain; if thought is in the brain it must be in the brain's substance and not in the motions which brain substance makes. But thought is not in the brain substance, for brain substance* without life, is quite unintelligent and dead. Thought is in the life-principle which animates the brain in the spirit substance, which is the real man. The brain does not think. The man thinks and expresses his thought through the brain. There is a spirit substance which thinks. Just as the spirit substance of man permeates his body, and thinks and knows in the body, so the Original Spirit Substance, God, permeates all nature and thinks and knows in nature. Nature is as intelligent as man yet knows more than man; nature knows all things. The All-Mind has been in touch with all things from the beginning and it contains all knowledge. Man's experience covers a few things, and these things man knows; but God's experience covers all the things that have happened since the creation, from the wreck of a planet or the passing of a comet to the fall of a sparrow. God knows all that is, all that has been, and all that will be. God is wrapped about us, enfolds us and presses upon us from every side. All the encyclopedias men have written are but trivial affairs compared to the vast knowledge held by the mind in which men live, move, and have their being. The truths men perceive by inspiration are thoughts held in his mind. If there were not thoughts men could not perceive them, for they would have no existence; and they could not exist as thoughts unless there is a mind for them to exist in; and a mind can be nothing else than a substance which thinks. Man is a thinking substance, a portion of the Cosmic Substance; but man is limited, while God has no limits. We are immersed in mind and that mind contains all knowledge and all truth. It is seeking to give us this knowledge, for God delights to give good gifts to his children. The prophets and seers and great men and women, past and present, were made great by what they received from God, not by what they were taught by men. This limitless reservoir of wisdom and power is open to you; you can draw upon it as you will, according to your needs. You can make yourself what you desire to be; you can do what you wish to do; you can have what you want.

The Science of Being Great
Chapter 5
Preparation

You can never become a great man or woman until you have overcome anxiety, worry, and fear. It is impossible for an anxious person, a worried one, or a fearful one to perceive truth. All things are distorted and thrown out of their proper relations by such mental states, and those who are in them cannot understand what God wants from them. If you are poor, or if you are anxious about business or financial matters, you are recommended to carefully study the first volume of this series, The Science of Getting Rich. It presents a solution, no matter how large or how complicated problems of this nature may seem to be. There is no reason for worry about financial affairs. Every person who wills to do so may rise above his want, have all he needs, and become rich. The same source from which you propose to draw mental development and spiritual power is at your service for the supply of all your material wants. Study this truth until it is fixed in your thoughts and until anxiety is banished from your mind; enter the Certain Way, which leads to material riches. Again, if you are anxious or worried about your health, realize it is possible for you to attain perfect health so that you may have sufficient strength for all that you wish to do and more. God stands ready to give you wealth, mental and spiritual power, and perfect health. Perfect health is yours for the asking, if you will only obey the simple laws of life and live properly. Conquer ill- health and cast out fear. But it is not enough to rise above financial and physical anxiety and worry; you must rise above moral evil-doing as well. Sound your inner consciousness now for the motives which actuate you and make sure they are right. You must cast out lust and cease to be ruled by appetite. You must begin to govern your appetite. You must eat only to satisfy hunger, never for gluttonous pleasure, and in all things you must make the flesh obey the spirit. You must lay aside greed and have no unworthy motive in your desire to become rich and powerful. It is legitimate and right to desire riches, if you want them for the sake of the soul, but not if you desire them for the lusts of the flesh. Cast out pride and vanity; have no thought of trying to rule over others or of outdoing them. This is a vital point; there is no temptation so insidious as the selfish desire to rule over others. Nothing so appeals to the average man or woman as to sit in the uppermost places at feasts and be respectfully saluted. To exercise some sort of control over others is the secret motive of every selfish person. The struggle for power over others is the battle of the competitive world, and you must rise above that world and its motives and aspirations and seek only for life. Cast out envy; you can have all that you want, and you need not envy any man what he has. Above all, see to it that you do not hold malice or enmity toward any one. Lay aside all narrow personal ambition and determine to seek the highest good and be swayed by no unworthy selfishness. Go over all the foregoing and set these moral temptations out of your heart one by one. Determine to keep them out. Then resolve that you will not only abandon all evil thought but that you will forsake all deeds, habits, and courses of action which do not commend themselves to your noblest ideals. This is of particular importance. Make this resolution with all the power of your soul. You are now ready for the next step toward greatness.

The Science of Being Great
Chapter 6
The Social Point of View

WITHOUT faith it is impossible to please God, and without faith it is impossible for you to become great. The distinguishing characteristic of all really great men and women is an unwavering faith. We see this in Abraham Lincoln during the dark days of the war; we see it in George Washington at Valley Forge; we see it in Stanley Livingstone, the crippled missionary, threading the mazes of the dark continent, his soul aflame with the determination to let in the light upon the accursed slave trade, which his soul abhorred; and in Frances Willard, in every man and woman who has attained a place on the muster roll of the great ones of the world. Faith—not a faith in one's self or in one s own powers but faith in God; in principle which upholds right, and which may be relied upon to give us the victory in due time. Without this faith it is impossible for any one of us to rise to real greatness. The man who has no faith in principle will always be a small man. Whether you have this faith or not depends upon your point of view. You must learn to see the world as something which is evolving and becoming; not as a finished work. Millions of years ago God worked with very low and crude forms of life; low and crude, yet each perfect after its kind. Higher and more complex organisms, animal and vegetable, appeared through the successive ages; the earth passed through stage after stage in its development, each stage perfect in itself, and to be succeeded by a higher one. What I wish you to note is that the so-called "lower organisms" are as perfect after their kind as the higher ones; that the world in the Eocene period was perfect for that period; it was perfect, but God's work was not finished. This is true of the world today. Physically, socially, and industrially it is all good, and it is all perfect. It is not complete anywhere or in any part, but so far as the handiwork of God has gone it is perfect.

THIS MUST BE YOUR POINT OF VIEW:
THAT THE WORLD AND ALL IT CONTAINS IS PERFECT, THOUGH NOT COMPLETED.

"All's right with the world." That is the great fact. There is nothing wrong with anything; there is nothing wrong with anybody. All the facts of life you must contemplate from this standpoint. There is nothing wrong with nature. Nature is a great advancing presence working beneficently for the happiness of all. All things in nature are good; it has no evil. It is not complete, for creation is still unfinished, but continues to give to man even more bountifully than it has in the past. Nature is a partial expression of God. It is perfect but not complete. The same can be said of human society and government even though there are trusts and combinations of capital and strikes and lockouts and so on. All these things are part of the forward movement and are incidental to the evolutionary process of completing society. When it is complete inharmonious interactions there cease; but it cannot be completed without them. J. P. Morgan is as necessary to the coming social order as the strange animals of the age of reptiles were to the life of the succeeding period, and just as these animals were perfect after their kind, so Morgan is perfect after his kind. Behold it is all very good. Consider government and industry as being perfect now and advancing rapidly toward being complete; then you will understand that there is nothing to fear, no cause for anxiety, nothing to worry about. Never complain of any of these things. They are perfect; this is the very best possible world for the stage of development man has reached. This will sound like rank folly to many, perhaps to most people. "What!" they will say, "are not child labor and the exploitation of men and women in filthy and unsanitary factories evil things? Are not saloons evil? Do you mean to say that we shall accept all this and call them good?" Child labor and similar things are no more evil than the manner of living, the habits, and practices of the cave dweller. His ways were those of the savage stage of man's growth, and for that stage they were perfect. Our industrial practices are those of the savage stage of industrial development, and they are also perfect. Nothing better is possible until we cease to be mental savages in industry and business, and become men and women. This can only come about by the rise of the whole race to a higher viewpoint. And this can only come about by the rise of such individuals here and there as are ready for the higher viewpoint. The cure for all these inharmonious relations lie not with the masters or employers but with the workers themselves. Whenever they reach a higher viewpoint, whenever they shall desire to do so, they can establish complete brotherhood and harmony in industry; they have the numbers and the power. They are getting now what they desire. Whenever they desire more in the way of a higher, purer, more harmonious life, they will receive more. True, they want more now, but they only want more of the things that make for animal enjoyment, and so industry remains in the savage, brutal, animal stage; when the workers begin to rise to the mental plane of living and ask for more of the things that make for the life of the mind and soul, industry will at once be raised above the plane of savagery and brutality. But it is perfect now upon its plane. Behold, it is all very good. So of saloons and dens of vice. If a majority of the people desire these things, it is right and necessary that they should have them. When a majority desire a world without such discord, they will create such a world. As long as men and women are on the plane of bestial thought and as long as the social order will be in part disorder it will show bestial manifestations. The people make society what it is, and as the people rise above the bestial thought, society will rise above the beastly in its manifestations. But a society which thinks in a bestial way must have saloons and dives. It is perfect after its kind, as the world was, in the Eocene period, and very good. All this does not prevent you from working for better things. You can work to complete an unfinished society instead of renovating a decaying one. You can work with a better heart and a more hopeful spirit. It will make an immense difference with your faith and spirit whether you look upon civilization as a good thing which is becoming better or as a bad and evil thing which is decaying. One viewpoint gives you an advancing and expanding mind and the other gives you a descending and decreasing mind. One viewpoint will make you grow greater and the other will inevitably cause you to grow smaller. One will enable you to work for the eternal things; to do large works in a great way toward the completing of all that is incomplete and inharmonious; and the other will make you a mere patchwork reformer, working almost without hope to save a few lost souls from what you will grow to consider a lost and doomed world. So you see it makes a vast difference to you. "All's right with the world. Nothing can possibly be wrong but my personal attitude and I will make that right. I will see the facts of nature and all the events, circumstances, and conditions of society, politics, government, and industry from the highest viewpoint. It is all perfect, though incomplete. It is all the handiwork of God. Behold, it is all very good."

The Science of Being Great
Chapter 7
The Individual Point of View

IMPORTANT as your point of view for the facts of social life are, it is of less concern than your viewpoint for your fellow man, acquaintances, friends, relatives, your immediate family, and, most of all, yourself. You must learn not to look upon the world as a lost and decaying thing but as a something perfect and glorious which is going on to a most beautiful completeness; and you must learn to see men and women not as lost and accursed things, but as perfect beings advancing to become complete. There are no "bad" or "evil" people. An engine which is on the rails pulling a heavy train is perfect after its kind, and it is good. The power of steam which drives it is good. Let a broken rail throw the engine into the ditch, and it does not become bad or evil by being so displaced; it is a perfectly good engine, but off the track. The power of steam which drives it into the ditch and wrecks it is not evil, but a perfectly good power. So that which is misplaced or applied in an incomplete or partial way is not evil, There are no evil people; there are perfectly good people who are off the track, but they do not need condemnation or punishment; they only need to get upon the rails again. That which is undeveloped or incomplete often appears to us as evil because of the way we have trained ourselves to think. The root of a bulb which shall produce a white lily is an unsightly thing; one might look upon it with disgust. But how foolish we should be to condemn the bulb for its appearance when we know the lily is within it. The root is perfect after its kind; it is a perfect but incomplete lily, and so we must learn to look upon every man and woman, no matter how unlovely in outward manifestation; they are perfect in their stage of being and they are becoming complete. Behold, it is all very good. Once we come into a comprehension of this fact and arrive at this point of view, we lose all desire to find fault with people, to judge them, criticize them, or condemn them. We no longer see men as trees walking, but our vision is complete. We have nothing but good words to say. It is all good; a great and glorious humanity coming to completeness. And in our association with men this puts us into an expansive and enlarging attitude of mind; we see them as great beings and we begin to deal with them and their affairs in a great way. But if we fall to the opposite point of view and see a lost and degenerate race we shrink into the contracting mind; and our dealings with men and their affairs will be in a small and contracted way. Remember to hold steadily to this point of view; if you do you cannot fail to begin at once to deal with your acquaintances and neighbors and with your own family as a great personality deals with men. This same viewpoint must be the one from which you regard yourself. You must always see yourself as a great advancing soul. Learn to say: "There is THAT in me of which I am made, which knows no imperfection, weakness, or sickness. The world is incomplete, but God in my own consciousness is both perfect and complete. Nothing can be wrong but my own personal attitude, and my own personal attitude can be wrong only when I disobey THAT which is within. I am a perfect vessel of G-d so far as I have gone, and I will press on to be complete, I will trust and not be afraid." When you are able to say this understandingly you will have lost all fear and you will be far advanced upon the road to the development of a great and powerful personality.

The Science of Being Great
Chapter 8
Idealization

YOU are a thinking center in original substance, and the thoughts of original substance have creative power; whatever is formed in its thought and held as a thought-form must come into existence as a visible and so-called material form and a thought-form held in thinking substance is a reality; it is a real thing, whether it has yet become visible to mortal eye or not. This is a fact that you should impress upon your understanding—that a thought held in thinking substance is a real thing; a form, and has actual existence, although it is not visible to you. You internally take the form in which you think of yourself; and you surround yourself with the invisible forms of those things with which you associate in your thoughts. If you desire a thing, picture it clearly and hold the picture steadily in mind until it becomes a definite thought-form; and if your practices are not such as to separate you from God, the thing you want will come to you in material form. It must do so in obedience to the law by which the universe was created. Make no thought-form of yourself in connection with disease or sickness, but form a conception of health. Make a thought-form of yourself as strong and hearty and perfectly well; impress this thought-form on creative intelligence, and if your practices are not in violation of the laws by which the physical body is built, your thought-form will become manifest in your flesh. This also is certain; it comes by obedience to law. Make a thought-form of yourself as you desire to be, and set your ideal as near to perfection as your imagination is capable of forming the conception. Let me illustrate: If a young law student wishes to become great, let him picture himself (while attending to the viewpoint, consecration, and identification, as previously directed) as a great lawyer, pleading his case with matchless eloquence and power before the judge and jury; as having an unlimited command of truth, of knowledge, and of wisdom. Let him picture himself as the great lawyer in every possible situation and contingency; while he is still only the student in all circumstances, let him never forget or fail to he the great lawyer in his thought-form of himself. As the thought-form grows more definite and habitual in his mind, the creative energies, both within and without, are set at work, he begins to manifest the form from within and all the essentials without, which go into the picture begin to be impelled toward him. He makes himself into the image and God works with him; nothing can prevent him from becoming what he wishes to he. In the same general way the music student pictures himself as performing perfect harmonies, and as delighting vast audiences; the actor forms the highest conception he is capable of in regard to his art, and applies this conception to himself. The farmer and the mechanic do exactly the same thing. Fix upon your ideal of what you wish to make of yourself; consider well and be sure

69

that you make the right choice; that is, the one which will be the most satisfactory to you in a general way. Do not pay too much attention to the advice or suggestions of those around you: do not believe that any one can know, better than yourself, what is right for you. Listen to what others have to say, but always form your own conclusions.

DO NOT LET OTHER PEOPLE DECIDE WHAT YOU ARE
TO BE.
BE WHAT YOU FEEL THAT YOU WANT TO BE.

Do not be misled by a false notion of obligation or duty. You can owe no possible obligation or duty to others which should prevent you from making the most of yourself. Be true to yourself, and you cannot then be false to any man. When you have fully decided what thing you want to be, form the highest conception of that thing that you are capable of imagining, and make that conception a thought-form. Hold that thought-form as a fact, as the real truth about yourself, and believe in it. Close your ears to all adverse suggestions. Never mind if people call you a fool and a dreamer. Dream on. Remember that Napoleon Bonaparte, the half-starved lieutenant, always saw himself as the general of armies and the master of France. He became an outward realization of what he held himself to be in his mind. Likewise will you. Attend carefully to all that has been said in the preceding chapters, and act as directed in the following ones, and you will become what you want to be.

The Science of Being Great
Chapter 9
Realization

IF you were to stop with the close of the last chapter, you would never become great. You would be a mere dreamer of dreams; a castle-builder. Too many do stop there. They do not understand the necessity for present action in realizing the vision and bringing the thought-form into manifestation. Two things are necessary. First, the making of the thought-form, and, second, the actual appropriation to yourself of all that goes into and around the thought-form. We have discussed the first, now we will proceed to give directions for the second. When you have made your thought-form, you are internally what you want to be. Next you must become externally what you want to be. You are already great within, but you are not yet doing the great things without. You cannot begin, on the instant, to do the great things; you cannot be before the world the great actor, or lawyer, or musician, or personality you know yourself to be; no one will entrust great things to you as yet for you have not made yourself known. But you can always begin to do small things in a great way. Here lies the whole secret. You can begin to be great today in your own home, in your store or office, on the street, everywhere; you can begin to make yourself known as great, and you can do this by doing everything you do in a great way. However small and common place, you must put the whole power of your soul into every act. You will reveal to your family, your friends, and neighbors who you really are. Do not brag or boast of yourself; do not go about telling people what a great person you are; simply live in a great way. No one will believe you if you tell him you are a great man, but no one can doubt your greatness if you show it in your actions. In your domestic circle be so just, so generous, so courteous, and so kind that your family, your wife, husband, children, brothers, and sisters will know that you are a great and noble soul. In all your relations with men be great, just, generous, courteous, and kind. The great ones are never otherwise. Make this your new attitude. Next, and most important, you must have absolute faith in your own perceptions of truth. Never act in haste or hurry; be deliberate in everything; wait until you feel that you know the true way. And when you do feel that you know the true way be guided by your own faith though all the world shall disagree with you. If you do not believe what God tells you in little things, you will never draw upon his wisdom and knowledge in larger things. When you feel deeply that a certain act is the right act, do it and have perfect faith that the consequences will be good. When you are deeply impressed that a certain thing is true, no matter what the appearances to the contrary may be, accept that thing as true and act accordingly. The one way to develop a perception of truth in large things is to trust absolutely to your present perception of truth in small things. Remember that you are seeking to develop this very power or faculty- the perception of truth; you are learning to understand what God wants from you. Nothing is great and nothing is small in the sight of the Omnipotence; he holds the sun in its place, but he also notes a sparrow's fall, and numbers the hairs of your head. God is as much interested in the little matters of everyday life as he is in the affairs of nations. You can perceive truth

71

about family and neighborhood affairs as well as about matters of statecraft. And the way to begin is to have perfect faith in the truth in these small matters, as it is revealed to you from day to day. When you feel deeply impelled to take a course which seems contrary to all reason and worldly judgment, take that course. Listen to the suggestions and advice of others, but always do what you feel deeply in the within to be the true thing to do. Rely with absolute faith, at all times, on your own perception of truth; but be sure that you listen to God - that you do not act in haste, fear, or anxiety. Rely upon your perception of truth in all the facts and circumstances of life. If you deeply feel that a certain man will be in a certain place on a certain day, go there with perfect faith to meet him; he will be there, no matter how unlikely it may seem. If you feel sure that certain people are making certain combinations, or doing certain things, act in the faith that they are doing those things. If you feel sure of the truth of any circumstance or happening, near or distant, past, present, or to come, trust in your perception. You may make occasional mistakes at first because of your imperfect understanding of the within; but you will soon be guided almost invariably right. Soon your family and friends will begin to defer, more and more, to your judgment and to be guided by you. Soon your neighbors and townsmen will be coming to you for counsel and advice; soon you will be recognized as one who is great in small things, and you will be called upon more and more to take charge of larger things. All that is necessary is to be guided absolutely, in all things, by your inner light, your perception of truth. Obey your soul, have perfect faith in yourself. Never think of yourself with doubt or distrust, or as one who makes mistakes.

The Science of Being Great
Chapter 10
Hurry and Habit

NO doubt you have many problems, domestic, social, physical, and financial, which seem to you to be pressing for instant solution. You have debts which must be paid, or other obligations which must be met; you are unhappily or inharmoniously placed, and feel that something must be done at once. Do not get into a hurry and act from superficial impulses. You can trust in G-d for the solution of all your personal riddles. There is no hurry. There is only God, and all is well with the world. There is an invincible power in you, and the same power is in the things you want. It is bringing them to you and bringing you to them. This is a thought that you must grasp, and hold continuously— that the same intelligence which is in you is in the things you desire. They are impelled toward you as strongly and decidedly as your desire impels you toward them. The tendency, therefore, of a steadily held thought must be to bring the things you desire to you and to group them around you. So long as you hold your thought and your faith right all must go well. Nothing can be wrong but your own personal attitude, and that will not be wrong if you trust and are not afraid. Hurry is a manifestation of fear; he who fears not has plenty of time. If you act with perfect faith in your own perceptions of truth, you will never be too late or too early; and nothing will go wrong. If things appear to be going wrong, do not get disturbed in mind; it is only in appearance. Nothing can go wrong in this world but yourself; and you can go wrong only by getting into the wrong mental attitude. Whenever you find yourself getting excited, worried, or into the mental attitude of hurry, sit down and think it over; play a game of some kind, or take a vacation. Go on a trip, and all will be right when you return. So surely as you find yourself in the mental attitude of haste, just so surely may you know that you are out of the mental attitude of greatness. Hurry and fear will instantly cut your connection with the universal mind; you will get no power, no wisdom, and no information until you are calm. And to fall into the attitude of hurry will check the action of the Principle of Power within you. Fear turns strength to weakness. Remember that poise and power are inseparably associated. The calm and balanced mind is the strong and great mind; the hurried and agitated mind is the weak one. Whenever you fall into the mental state of hurry you may know that you have lost the right viewpoint; you are beginning to look upon the world, or some part of it, as going wrong. At such times read Chapter Six of this book; consider the fact that this work is perfect, now, with all that it contains. Nothing is going wrong; nothing can be wrong; be poised, be calm, be cheerful; have faith in God. Regarding habit. It is probable that your greatest difficulty will be to overcome your old habitual ways of thought and to form new habits. The world is ruled by habit. Kings, tyrants, masters, and plutocrats hold their positions solely because the people have come to habitually accept them. Things are as they are only because people have formed the habit of accepting them as they are. When the people change their habitual thought about governmental, social, and industrial institutions, they will change the institutions. Habit rules us all. You have formed, perhaps, the habit of thinking of yourself as a common person, as one of a limited ability, or as being more or less of

73

a failure. Whatever you habitually think yourself to be, that you are. You must form, now, a greater and better habit; you must form a conception of yourself as a being of limitless power, and habitually think that you are that being. It is the habitual, not the periodical thought that decides your destiny. It will avail you nothing to sit apart for a few moments several times a day to affirm that you are great, if during all the balance of the day, while you are about your regular vocation, you think of yourself as not great. No amount of praying or affirmation will make you great if you still habitually regard yourself as being small. The use of prayer and affirmation is to change your habit of thought. Any act, mental or physical, often repeated, becomes a habit. The purpose of mental exercises is to repeat certain thoughts over and over until the thinking of those thoughts becomes constant and habitual. The thoughts we continually repeat become convictions. What you must do is to repeat the new thought of yourself until it is the only way in which you think of yourself. Habitual thought, and not environment or circumstance, has made you what you are. Every person has some central idea or thought-form of himself, and by this idea he classifies and arranges all his facts and external relationships. You are classifying your facts either according to the idea that you are a great and strong person, or according to the idea that you are limited, common, or weak. If the latter is the case you must change your central idea. Get a new mental picture of yourself. Do not try to become great by repeating mere strings of words or superficial formulas; but repeat over and over the THOUGHT of your own power and ability until you classify external facts, and decide your place everywhere by this idea. A mental exercise and further directions on this point follow in another chapter.

The Science of Being Great
Chapter 11
Thought

GREATNESS is attained only by the thinking of great thoughts. No man can become great in outward personality until he is great internally; and no man can be great internally until he THINKS. No amount of education, reading, or study can make you great without thought; but thought can make you great with very little study. There are altogether too many people who are trying to make something of themselves by reading books without thinking; all will fail. You are not mentally developed by what you read, but by what you think about what you read. Thinking is the hardest and most exhausting of all labor; and hence many people shrink from it. God has formed us so that we are continuously impelled to thought; we must either think or engage in some activity to escape thought. The headlong, continuous chase for pleasure in which most people spend all their leisure time is only an effort to escape thought. If they are alone, or if they have nothing amusing to take their attention, as a novel to read or a show to see, they must think; and to escape from thinking they resort to novels, shows, and all the endless devices of the purveyors of amusement. Most people spend the greater part of their leisure time running away from thought hence they are where they are. We never move forward until we begin to think. Read less and think more. Read about great things and think about great questions and issues. We have at the present time few really great figures in the political life of our country; our politicians are a petty lot. There is no Lincoln, no Webster, no Clay, Calhoun, or Jackson. Why? Because our present statesmen deal only with sordid and petty issues - questions of dollars and cents, of expediency and party success, of material prosperity without regard to ethical right. Thinking along these lines does not call forth great souls. The statesmen of Lincoln's time and previous times dealt with questions of eternal truth; of human rights and justice. Men thought upon great themes; they thought great thoughts, and they became great men. Thinking, not mere knowledge or information, makes personality. Thinking is growth; you cannot think without growing. Every thought engenders another thought. Write one idea and others will follow until you have written a page. You cannot fathom your own mind; it has neither bottom nor boundaries. Your first thoughts may be crude; but as you go on thinking you will use more and more of yourself; you will quicken new brain cells into activity and you will develop new faculties. Heredity, environment, circumstances,—all things must give way before you if you practice sustained and continuous thought. But, on the other hand, if you neglect to think for yourself and only use other people's thought, you will never know what you are capable of; and you will end by being incapable of anything. There can be no real greatness without original thought. All that a man does outwardly is the expression and completion of his inward thinking. No action is possible without thought, and no great action is possible until a great thought has preceded it. Action is the second form of thought, and personality is the materialization of thought. Environment is the result of thought; things group themselves or arrange themselves around you according to your thought. There is, as Emerson says, some central idea or conception of yourself by which all the facts

75

of your life are arranged and classified. Change this central idea and you change the arrangement or classification of all the facts and circumstances of your life. You are what you are because you think as you do; you are where you are because you think as you do. You see then the immense importance of thinking about the great essentials set forth in the preceding chapters. You must not accept them in any superficial way; you must think about them until they are a part of your central idea. Go back to the matter of the point of view and consider, in all its bearings, the tremendous thought that you live in a perfect world among perfect people, and that nothing can possibly be wrong with you but your own personal attitude. Think about all this until you fully realize all that it means to you. Consider that this is God's world and that it is the best of all possible worlds; that He has brought it thus far toward completion by the processes of organic, social, and industrial evolution, and that it is going on to greater completeness and harmony. Consider that God is one great, perfect, intelligent Principle of Life and Power, causing all the changing phenomena of the cosmos. Think about all this until you see that it is true, and until you comprehend how you should live and act as a citizen of such a perfect whole. Next, think of the wonderful truth that this great Intelligence is in you; it is your own intelligence. It is an Inner Light impelling you toward the right thing and the best thing, the greatest act, and the highest happiness. It is a Principle of Power in you, giving you all the ability and genius there is. Great thoughts will manifest in a great personality. Think well of all this, and then you are ready to act.

The Science of Being Great
Chapter 12
Acting at Home

DO not merely think that you are going to become great; think that you are great now. Do not think that you will begin to act in a great way at some future time; begin now. Do not think that you will act in a great way when you reach a different environment; act in a great way where you are now. Do not think that you will begin to act in a great way when you begin to deal with great things; begin to deal in a great way with small things. Do not think that you will begin to be great when you get among more intelligent people, or among people who understand you better; begin now to deal in a great way with the people around you. If you are not in an environment where there is scope for your best powers and talents you can move in due time; but meanwhile you can be great where you are. Lincoln was as great when he was a backwoods lawyer as when he was President. As a backwoods lawyer he did common things in a great way, and that made him President. Had he waited until he reached Washington to begin to be great, he would have remained unknown. You are not made great by the location in which you happen to be, nor by the things with which you may surround yourself. You are not made great by what you receive from others, and you can never manifest greatness so long as you depend on others. You will manifest greatness only when you begin to stand alone. Dismiss all thought of reliance on externals, whether things, books, or people. As Emerson said, "Shakespeare will never be made by the study of Shakespeare." Shakespeare will be made by the thinking of Shakespearean thoughts. Never mind how the people around you, including those of your own household, may treat you. That has nothing at all to do with your being great; it cannot hinder you from being great. People may neglect you and be unthankful and unkind in their attitude toward you. Does that prevent you from being great in your manner and attitude toward them? Would God be great if he should go away and sulk because people were unthankful and did not appreciate him?

Treat the unthankful and the evil in a great and perfectly kind way, just as God does.

Do not talk about your greatness; you are really, in essential nature, no greater than those around you. You may have entered upon a way of living and thinking which they have not yet found, but they are perfect on their own plane of thought and action. You are entitled to no special honor or consideration for your greatness. You will fall into the boastful attitude if you see other people's shortcomings and failures and compare them with your own virtues and successes; and if you fall into the boastful attitude of mind, you will cease to be great, and become small. Think of yourself as a perfect being among perfect beings, and meet every person as an equal, not as either a superior or an inferior. Give yourself no airs; great people never do. Ask no honors and seek for no recognition; honors and recognition will come fast enough if you are entitled to them. Begin at home. It is a great person who can always be poised, assured, calm, and perfectly kind and considerate at home. If your manner and attitude in your own family are always the best you can think, you will soon become the one on whom all the others will rely. You will be a tower of strength and a support in time of trouble. You will be loved and appreciated. At the same time do not make the mistake of throwing yourself away in the service of others. The great person respects himself; he serves and helps, but he is never slavishly servile. You cannot help your family by being a slave to them, or by doing for them those things which by right they should do for themselves. You do a person an injury when you wait on him too much. The selfish and exacting are a great deal better off if their exactions are denied. The ideal world is not one where there are a lot of people being waited on by other people; it is a world where everybody waits on himself. Meet all demands, selfish and otherwise, with perfect kindness and consideration; but do not allow yourself to be made a slave to the whims, caprices, exactions, or slavish desires of any member of your family. To do so is not great, and it works an injury to the other party. Do not become uneasy over the failures or mistakes of any member of your family, and feel that you must interfere. Do not be disturbed if others seem to be going wrong, and feel that you must step in and set them right. Remember that every person is perfect on his own plane; you cannot improve on the work of G-d. Do not meddle with the personal habits and practices of others, though they are your nearest and dearest; these things are none of your business. Nothing can be wrong but your own personal attitude; make that right and you will know that all else is right. You are a truly great soul when you can live with those who do things which you do not do, and yet refrain from either criticism or interference. Do the things which are right for you to do, and believe that every member of your family is doing the things which are right for him. Nothing is wrong with anybody or anything; behold, it is all very good. Do not be enslaved by any one else, but be just as careful that you do not enslave any one else to your own notions of what is right. Think, and think deeply and continuously; be perfect in your kindness and consideration. This is the way to being great in your own home.

The Science of Being Great
Chapter 13
Action Abroad

THE rules which apply to your action at home must apply to your action everywhere. Never forget for an instant that this is a perfect world. You are as great as the greatest, but all are your equals. Rely absolutely on your perception of truth. Trust to the inner light rather than to reason, but be sure that your perception comes from the inner light; act in poise and calmness; be still and attend on God. Your identification of yourself with the Al-Mighty will give you all the knowledge you need for guidance in any contingency which may arise in your own life or in the lives of others. It is only necessary that you should be supremely calm, and rely upon the eternal wisdom which is within you. If you act in poise and faith, your judgment will always be right, and you will always know exactly what to do. Do not hurry or worry; remember Lincoln in the dark days of the war. James Freeman Clarke relates that after the battle of Fredericksburg, Lincoln alone furnished a supply of faith and hope for the nation. Hundreds of leading men, from all parts of the country, went sadly into his room and came out cheerful and hopeful. They had stood face to face with the Highest, and had seen God in this lank, ungainly, patient man, although they knew it not. Have perfect faith in yourself and in your own ability to cope with any combination of circumstances that may arise. Do not be disturbed if you are alone; if you need Mends they will be brought to you at the right time. Do not be disturbed if you feel that you are ignorant; the information that you need will be furnished you when it is time for you to have it. That which is in you impelling you forward is in the things and people you need, impelling them toward you. If there is a particular man you need to know, he will be introduced to you; if there is a particular book you need to read it will be placed in your hands at the right time. All the knowledge you need will come to you from both external and internal sources. Your information and your talents will always be equal to the requirements of the occasion. As soon as you awaken and begin to use your mental faculties in a great way you will apply power to the development of your brain; new cells will be created and dormant cells quickened into activity, and your brain will be qualified as a perfect instrument for your mind. Do not try to do great things until you are ready to go about them in a great way. If you undertake to deal with great matters in a small way— that is, from a low viewpoint or with incomplete consecration and wavering faith and courage—you will fail. Do not be in a hurry to get to the great things. Doing great things will not make you great, but becoming great will certainly lead you to the doing of great things. Begin to be great where you are and in the things you do every day. Do not be in haste to be found out or recognized as a great personality. Do not be disappointed if men do not nominate you for office within a month after you begin to practice what you read in this book. Great people never seek for recognition or applause; they are not great because they want to be paid for being so. Greatness is reward enough for itself; the joy of being something and of knowing that you are advancing is the greatest of all joys possible to man. If you begin in your own family, as described in the preceding chapter, and then assume the same mental attitude with your neighbors, friends, and those you meet in business, you will soon find that people are beginning to depend on you. Your advice will be sought, and a constantly increasing number of people will look to you for strength and inspiration, and rely upon your judgment. Here, as in the home, you must avoid meddling with other people's affairs. Help all who come to you, but do not go about officiously endeavoring to set other people right. Mind your own business. It is no part of your mission in life to correct people's morals, habits, or practices. Lead a great life, doing all things with a great spirit and in a great way. If your neighbor wishes to smoke or drink, it is his business; it is none of yours until he consults you about it. If you lead a great life and do no preaching, you will save a thousand times as many souls as one who leads a small life and preaches continuously. If you hold the right viewpoint of the world, others will find it out and be impressed by it through your daily conversation and practice. Do not try to convert others to your point of view, except by holding it and living accordingly. If your dedication is perfect you do not need to tell any one; it will speedily become apparent to all that you are guided by a higher principle than the average man or woman. If your identification with God is complete, you do not need to explain the fact to others; it will become self-evident. To become known as a great personality, you have nothing to do but to live. Do not imagine that you must go charging about the world like Don Quixote, tilting at windmills, and overturning things in general, in order to demonstrate that you are somebody. Do not go hunting for big things to do. Live a great life where you are, and in the daily work you have to do, and greater works will surely find you out. Big things will come to you, asking to be done. Be so impressed with the value of a man that you treat even a beggar or the tramp with the most distinguished consideration. All is God. Every man and woman is perfect. Do not save all your consideration for the poor; the millionaire is as good as the tramp. This is a perfectly good world, and there is not a person or thing extra in it but it is exactly right; be sure that you keep this in mind in dealing with things and men. Form your mental vision of yourself with care. Make the thought-form of yourself as you wish to be, and hold this with the faith that it is being realized, and with the purpose to realize it completely. Begin thus and continue thus, and your development will be great and rapid.

The Science of Being Great
Chapter 14
Some Further Explanations

WE go back here to the matter of the point of view, for, besides being vitally important, it is the one which is likely to give the student the most trouble. We have been trained, partly by mistaken religious teachers, to look upon the world as being like a wrecked ship, storm-driven upon a rocky coast; utter destruction is inevitable at the end, and the most that can be done is to rescue, perhaps, a few of the crew. This view teaches us to consider the world as essentially bad and growing worse; and to believe that existing discords and inharmonious interactions must continue and intensify until the end. It robs us of hope for society, government, and humanity, and gives us a decreasing outlook and contracting mind. This is all wrong. The world is not wrecked. It is like a magnificent steamer with the engines in place and the machinery in perfect order. The bunkers are full of coal, and the ship is amply provisioned for the cruise; there is no lack of any good thing. Every provision the Omniscience could devise has been made for the safety, comfort, and happiness of the crew; the steamer is out on the high seas tacking hither and thither because no one has yet learned the right course to steer. We are learning to steer, and in due time will come grandly into the harbor of perfect harmony. The world is good, and growing better. Existing discords and inharmonious relation are but the movement of the ship incidental to our own imperfect steering; they will all be removed in due time. This view gives us an positive outlook and an expanding mind; it enables us to think largely of society and of ourselves, and to do things in a great way. Furthermore, we see that nothing can be wrong with such a world or with any part of it, including our own affairs. If it is all moving on toward completion, then it is not going wrong; and as our own personal affairs are a part of the whole, they are not going wrong. You and all that you are concerned with are moving on toward completeness. Nothing can check this forward movement but yourself; and you can only check it by assuming a mental attitude which is at cross purposes with the mind of God. You have nothing to keep right but yourself; if you keep yourself right, nothing can possibly go wrong with you, and you can have nothing to fear. No business or other disaster can come upon you if your personal attitude is right, for you are a part of that which is increasing and advancing, and you must increase and advance with it. Moreover your thought-form will be mostly shaped according to your viewpoint of the cosmos. If you see the world as a lost and ruined thing you will see yourself as a part of it, and as partaking of its sins and weaknesses. If your outlook for the world as a whole is hopeless, your outlook for yourself cannot be hopeful. If you see the world as declining toward its end, you cannot see yourself as advancing. Unless you think well of all the works of God you cannot really think well of yourself, and unless you think well of yourself you can never become great. I repeat that your place in life, including your material environment, is determined by the thought-form you habitually hold of yourself. When you make a thought-form of yourself you can hardly fail to form in your mind a corresponding environment If you think of yourself as an incapable, inefficient person, you will think of yourself with poor or cheap surroundings. Unless you think well of yourself you will be sure to picture yourself in a more or less poverty stricken environment. These thoughts, habitually held, become invisible forms in the surrounding mind-stuff, and are with you continually. In due time, by the regular action of the eternal creative energy, the invisible thought-forms are produced in material stuff, and you are surrounded by your own thoughts made into material things. View nature as a great living and advancing presence, and see human society in exactly the same way. It is all one, coming from one source, and it is all good. All the constituents of God are parts of yourself.

The Science of Being Great
Chapter 15
More About Thought

GIVE place here to some further consideration of thought. You will never become great until your own thoughts make you great, and therefore it is of the first importance that you should THINK. You will never do great things in the external world until you think great things in the internal world; and you will never think great things until you think about truth; about the verities. To think great things you must be absolutely sincere; and to be sincere you must know that your intentions are right. Insincere or false thinking is never great, however logical and brilliant it may be. The first and most important step is to seek the truth about human relations; to know what you ought to be to other men, and what they ought to be to you. This brings you back to the search for a right viewpoint. You should study organic and social evolution. Read Darwin and Walter Thomas Mills, and when you read, THINK; think the whole matter over until you see the world of things and men in the right way. THINK about what God is doing until you can SEE what he is doing. Your next step is to think yourself into the right personal attitude. Your viewpoint tells you what the right attitude is, and obedience to the soul puts you into it. It is only by making a complete consecration of yourself to the highest that is within you that you can attain to sincere thinking. So long as you know you are selfish in your aims, or dishonest or crooked in any way in your intentions or practices, your thinking will be false and your thoughts will have no power. THINK about the way you are doing things; about all your intentions, purposes, and practices, until you know that they are right. The fact of his own complete unity with God is one that no person can grasp without deep and sustained thinking. Any one can accept the proposition in a superficial way, but to feel and realize a vital comprehension of it is another matter. It is easy to think of going outside of yourself to meet God, but it is not so easy to think of going inside yourself to meet G-d. But God is there. It is a tremendous thing, that all you need is already within you; that you do not have to consider how to get the power to do what you want to do or to make yourself what you want to be. You have only to consider how to use the power you have in the right way. And there is nothing to do but to begin. Use your perception of truth; you can see some truth today; live fully up to that and you will see more truth tomorrow. To rid yourself of the old false ideas you will have to think a great deal about the value of men—the greatness and worth of a human soul. You must cease from looking at human mistakes and look at successes; cease from seeing faults and see virtues. You can no longer look upon men and women as lost and ruined beings who are descending into hell; you must come to regard them as shining souls who are ascending toward heaven. It will require some exercise of will power to do this, but this is the legitimate use of the will—to decide what you will think about and how you will think. The function of the will is to direct thought. Think about the good side of men; the lovely, attractive part, and exert your will in refusing to think of anything else in connection with them. I know of no one who has attained to so much on this one point as Eugene V. Debs, twice the Socialist candidate for president of the United States. Mr. Debs reverences humanity. No

appeal for help is ever made to him in vain. No one receives from him an unkind or censorious word. You cannot come into his presence without being made sensible of his deep and kindly personal interest in you. No one, whether millionaire, grimy workingman, or toil worn woman, meets him without receiving the radiant warmth of a brotherly affection that is sincere and true. No ragged child speaks to him on the street without receiving instant and tender recognition. Debs loves men. This has made him the leading figure in a great movement, the beloved hero of a million hearts, and will give him a deathless name. It is a great thing to love men so and it is only achieved by thought. Nothing can make you great but thought. "We may divide thinkers into those who think for themselves and those who think through others. The latter are the rule and the former the exception. The first are original thinkers in a double sense, and egotists in the noblest meaning of the word." — Sehopenhauer. "The key to every man is his thought. Sturdy and defiant though he look he has a helm which he obeys, which is the idea after which all his facts are classified. He can only be reformed by showing him a new idea which commands his own." —Emerson. "All truly wise thoughts have been thought already thousands of times; but to make them really ours we must think them over again honestly till they take root in our personal expression."—Goethe. "All that a man is outwardly is but the expression and completion of his inward thought. To work effectively he must think clearly. To act nobly he must think nobly." —Channing. "Great men are they who see that spirituality is stronger than any material force; that thoughts rule the world." —Emerson. "Some people study all their lives, and at their death they have learned everything except to think." —Domergue. "It is the habitual thought that frames itself into our life. It affects us even more than our intimate social relations do. Our confidential friends have not so much to do in shaping our lives as the thoughts have which we harbor?' —J, W. Teal. "When God lets loose a great thinker on this planet, then all things are at risk. There is not a piece of science but its flank may be turned tomorrow; nor any literary reputation or the so-called eternal names of fame that may not be refused and condemned," — Emerson.
Think! Think!! THINK!!!

The Science of Being Great
Chapter 16
A View of Evolution

BUT how shall we avoid throwing ourselves into altruistic work if we are surrounded by poverty, ignorance, suffering, and every appearance of misery as very many people are? Those who live where the withered hand of want is thrust upon them from every side appealingly for aid must find it hard to refrain from continuous giving. Again, there are social and other irregularities, injustices done to the weak, which fire generous souls with an almost irresistible desire to set things right. We want to start a crusade; we feel that the wrongs will never be righted until we give ourselves wholly to the task. In all this we must fall back upon the point of view. We must remember that this is not a bad world but a good world in the process of becoming. Beyond all doubt there was a time when there was no life upon this earth. The testimony of geology to the fact that the globe was once a ball of burning gas and molten rock, clothed about with boiling vapors, is indisputable. And we do not know how life could have existed under such conditions; that seems impossible. Geology tells us that later on a crust formed, the globe copied and hardened, the vapors condensed and became mist or fell in rain. The cooled surface crumbled into soil; moisture accumulated, ponds and seas were gathered together, and at last somewhere in the water or on the land appeared something that was alive. It is reasonable to suppose that this first life was in single-celled organisms, but behind these cells was the insistent urge of God seeking expression. And soon organisms having too much life to express themselves with one cell had two cells and then many, and still more life was poured into them. Multiple-celled organisms were formed; plants, trees, vertebrates, and mammals, many of them with strange shapes, but all were perfect after their kind as everything is that God makes. No doubt there were crude and almost monstrous forms of both animal and plant life; but everything filled its purpose in its day and it was all very good. Then another day came, the great day of the evolutionary process, a day when the morning stars sang together and the sons of God shouted for joy to behold the beginning of the end, for man, the object aimed at from the beginning, had appeared upon the scene. An ape-like being, little different from the beasts around him in appearance but infinitely different in his capacity for growth and thought. Art and beauty, architecture and song, poetry and music, all these were unrealized possibilities in that ape man's soul. And for his time and kind he was very good. From the day the first man appeared God began to work IN men, putting more and more of himself into each succeeding generation, urging them on to larger achievements and to better conditions, social, governmental, and domestic. Those who looking back into ancient history see the awful conditions which existed, the barbarities, idolatries, and sufferings, and reading about God in connection with these things are disposed to feel that he was cruel and unjust to man, should pause to think. And it could only be accomplished by the successive developments of the various powers and possibilities latent in the human brain. Naturally the cruder and more animal-like part of for the thoughtful mind to answer. God desired to express himself, to live in form, and not only that, but to live in a form through which he could express

85

himself on the highest moral and spiritual plane. God wanted to evolve a form in which he could live as a god and manifest himself as a god. This was the aim of the evolutionary force. The ages of warfare, bloodshed, suffering, injustice, and cruelty were tempered in many ways with love and justice as time advanced. And this was developing the brain of man to a point where it should be capable of giving full expression to the love and justice of God. The end is not yet; God aims not at the perfection of a few choice specimens for exhibition, like the large berries at the top of the box, but at the glorification of the race. The time will come when the Kingdom of G-d shall be established on earth; the time foreseen by the dreamer of the Isle of Patmos, when there shall be no more crying, neither shall there be any more pain, for the former things are all passed away, and there shall be no night there.

The Science of Being Great
Chapter 17
Serving God

I HAVE brought you thus far through the two preceding chapters with a view to finally settling the question of duty. This is one that puzzles and perplexes very many people who are earnest and sincere, and gives them a great deal of difficulty in its solution. When they start out to make something of themselves and to practice the science of being great, they find themselves necessarily compelled to rearrange many of their relationships. There are friends who perhaps must be alienated, there are relatives who misunderstand and who feel that they are in some way being slighted; the really great man is often considered selfish by a large circle of people who are connected with him and who feel that he might bestow upon them more benefits than he does. The question at the outset is: Is it my duty to make the most of myself regardless of everything else? Or shall I wait until I can do so without any friction or without causing loss to any one? This is the question of duty to self vs. duty to others. One's duty to the world has been thoroughly discussed in the preceding pages and I give some consideration now to the idea of duty to God. An immense number of people have a great deal of uncertainty, not to say anxiety, as to what they ought to do for God. The amount of work and service that is done for him in these United States in the way of religious work and so on is enormous. An immense amount of human energy is expended in what is called serving God. I propose to consider briefly what serving God is and how a man may serve God best, and I think I shall be able to make plain that the conventional idea as to what constitutes service to God is all wrong. When Moses went down into Egypt to bring out the Hebrews from bondage, his demand upon Pharaoh, in the name of God, was, "Let the people go that they may serve me." He led them out into the wilderness and there instituted a new form of worship which has led many people to suppose that worship constitutes the service of God, although later God himself distinctly declared that he cared nothing for ceremonies, burned offerings, or oblation. God does not lack anything that men may do for him with their hands or bodies or voices. The view of evolution which we have taken shows God seeking expression through man. Through all the successive ages in which his spirit has urged man up the height, God has gone on seeking expression. Every generation of men is more Godlike than the preceding generation. Every generation of men demands more in the way of fine homes, pleasant surroundings, congenial work, rest, travel, and opportunity for study than the preceding generation. I have heard some shortsighted economists argue that the working people of today ought surely to be fully contented because their condition is so much better than that of the workingman two hundred years ago who slept in a windowless hut on a floor covered with rushes in company with his pigs. If that man had all that he was able to use for the living of all the life he knew how to live, he was perfectly content, and if he had lack he was not contented. The man of today has a comfortable home and very many things, indeed, that were unknown a short period back in the past, and if he has all that he can use for the living of all the life he can imagine, he will be content. But he is not content. God has lifted the race so far that any common man can picture a better and more desirable life than he is able to live under existing conditions. And so long as this is true, so long as a man can think and clearly picture to himself a more desirable life, he will be discontented with the life he has to live, and rightly so. That discontent is God urging men on to more desirable conditions. It is God who seeks expression in the race. The only service you can render God is to give expression to what he is trying to give the world, through you. The only service you can render God is to make the very most of yourself in order that God may live in you to the utmost of your possibilities. In a former work of this series, The Science of Getting Rich, I refer to the little boy at the piano, the music in whose soul could not find expression through his untrained hands. This is a good illustration of the way the God is over, about, around, and in all of us, seeking to do great things with us, so soon as we will train our hands and feet, our minds, brains, and bodies to do his service. Your first duty is to God, to yourself, and to the world is to make yourself as great a personality, in every way, as you possibly can. And that, it seems to me, disposes of the question of duty. There are one or two other things which might be disposed of in closing this chapter. I have written of opportunity in a preceding chapter. I have said, in a general way, that it is within the power of every man to become great, just as in The Science of Getting Rich I declared that it is within the power of every man to become rich. But these sweeping generalizations need qualifying. There are men who have such materialistic minds that they are absolutely incapable of comprehending the philosophy set forth in these books. There is a great mass of men and women who have lived and worked until they are practically incapable of thought along these lines; and they cannot receive the message. Something may be done for them by demonstration, that is, by living the life before them. But that is the only way they can be aroused. The world needs demonstration more than it needs teaching. For this mass of people our duty is to become as great in personality as possible in order that they may see and desire to do likewise. It is our duty to make ourselves great for their sakes, so that we may help prepare the world that the next generation shall have better conditions for thought. One other point. I am frequently written to by people who wish to make something of themselves and to move out into the world, but who are hampered by home ties, having others more or less dependent upon them, whom they fear would suffer if left alone. In general I advise such people to move out fearlessly, and to make the most of themselves. If there is a loss at home it will be only temporary and apparent, for in a little while, you will be able to take better care of your dependents than you have ever done before.

The Science of Being Great
Chapter 18
A Mental Exercise

THE purpose of mental exercises must not be misunderstood. There is no virtue in charms or formulated strings of words; there is no short cut to development by repeating prayers or incantations. A mental exercise is an exercise, not in repeating words, but in the thinking of certain thoughts. The phrases that we repeatedly hear become convictions, as Goethe says; and the thoughts that we repeatedly think become habitual, and make us what we are. The purpose in taking a mental exercise is that you may think certain thoughts repeatedly until you form a habit of thinking them; then they will be your thoughts all the time. Taken in the right way and with an understanding of their purpose, mental exercises are of great value; but taken as most people take them they are worse than useless. The thoughts embodied in the following exercise are the ones you want to think. You should take the exercise once or twice daily, but you should think the thoughts continuously. That is, do not think them twice a day for a stated time and then forget them until it is time to take the exercise again. The exercise is to impress you with the material for continuous thought. Take a time when you can have from twenty minutes to half an hour secure from interruption, and proceed first to make yourself physically comfortable. Lie at ease in a Morris chair, or on a couch, or in bed; it is best to lie flat on your back. If you have no other time, take the exercise on going to bed at night and before rising in the morning. First let your attention travel over your body from the crown of your head to the soles of your feet, relaxing every muscle as you go. Relax completely. And next, get physical and other ills off your mind. Let the attention pass down the spinal cord and out over the nerves to the extremities, and as you do so think:— "My nerves are in perfect order all over my body. They obey my will, and I have great nerve force." Next bring your attention to the lungs and think:— "I am breathing deeply and quietly, and the air goes into every cell of my lungs, which are in perfect condition. My blood is purified and made clean." Next, to the heart:— "My heart is beating strongly and steadily, and my circulation is perfect, even to the extremities.' Next, to the digestive system:— "My stomach and bowels perform their work perfectly. My food is digested and assimilated and my body rebuilt and nourished. My liver, kidneys, and bladder each perform their several functions without pain or strain; I am perfectly well. My body is resting, my mind is quiet, and my soul is at peace. "I have no anxiety about financial or other matters. God, who is within me, is also in all things I want, impelling them toward me; all that I want is already given to me. I have no anxiety about my health, for I am perfectly well. I have no worry or fear whatever. "I rise above all temptation to moral evil. I cast out all greed, selfishness, and narrow personal ambition; I do not hold envy, malice, or enmity toward any living soul. I will follow no course of action which is not in accord *with my highest ideals. I am right and I will do right." VIEWPOINT. All is right with the world. It is perfect and advancing to completion. I will contemplate the facts of social, political, and industrial life only from this high viewpoint. Behold, it is all very good. I will see all human beings, all my acquaintances, friends, neighbors, and the members of my own household in the same way. They are all good. Nothing is wrong with the universe; nothing can he wrong but my own personal attitude, and henceforth I keep that right. My whole trust is in God. I will search within for the pure idea of right in all things, and when I find it I will express it in my outward life. I will abandon everything I have outgrown for the best I can think. I will have the highest thoughts concerning all my relationships, and my manner and action shall express these thoughts. I surrender my body to be ruled by my mind; I yield my mind to the dominion of my soul, and I give my soul to the guidance of God. IDEALIZATION. Form a mental picture of yourself as you want to be, and at the greatest height your imagination can picture. Dwell upon this for some little time, holding the thought: "This is what I really am; it is a picture of my own perfect and advancing to completion. I will contemplate the facts of social, political, and industrial life only from this high viewpoint. Behold, it is all very good. I will see all human beings, all my acquaintances, friends, neighbors, and the members of my own household in the same way. They are all good. Nothing is wrong with the universe; nothing can he wrong but my own personal attitude, and henceforth I keep that right. My whole trust is in God. IDEALIZATION. Form a mental picture of yourself as you want to be, and at the greatest height your imagination can picture. Dwell upon this for some little time, holding the thought: "This is what I really am; it is a picture of my own soul. I am this now in soul, and I am becoming this in outward manifestation. REALIZATION. I appropriate to myself the power to become what I want to be, and to do what I want to do. I exercise creative energy; all the power there is mine. I will arise and go forth with power and perfect confidence; I will do mighty works in the strength of the Lord, my G-d. I will trust and not fear, for God is with me.

The Science of Being Great
Chapter 19
A Summary of The Science of Being GREAT

ALL men are made of the one intelligent substance, and therefore all contain the same essential powers and possibilities. Greatness is equally inherent in all, and may be manifested by all. Every person may become great. Every constituent of God is a constituent of man. Man may overcome both heredity and circumstances by exercising the inherent creative power of the soul. If he is to become great, the soul must act, and must rule the mind and the body. Man's knowledge is limited, and he falls into error through ignorance; to avoid this he must connect his soul with Universal Spirit. Universal Spirit is the intelligent substance from which all things come; it is in and through all things. All things are known to this universal mind, and man can so unite himself with it as to enter into all knowledge. To do this man must cast out of himself everything which separates him from God. He must will to live the divine life, and he must rise above all moral temptations; he must forsake every course of action that is not in accord with his highest ideals. He must reach the right viewpoint, recognizing that God is all, in all, and that there is nothing wrong. He must see that nature, society, government, and industry are perfect in their present stage, and advancing toward completion; and that all men and women everywhere are good and perfect. He must know that all is right with the world, and unite with God for the completion of the perfect work. It is only as man sees God as the Great Advancing Presence in all, and good in all, that he can rise to real greatness. He must dedicate himself to the service of the highest that is within himself, obeying the voice of the soul. There is an Inner Light in every man which continuously impels him toward the highest, and he must he guided by this light if he would become great. He must have absolute faith in his own perceptions of truth, And begin at home to act upon these perceptions. As he sees the true and right course in small things, he must take that course. He must cease to act unthinkingly, and begin to think; and he must be sincere in his thought. He must form a mental conception of himself at the highest, and hold this conception until it is his habitual thought-form of himself. This thought-form he must keep continuously in view. He must outwardly realize and express that thought-form in his actions. He must do everything that he does in a great way. In dealing with his family, his neighbors, acquaintances, and friends, he must make every act an expression of his ideal. The man who reaches the right viewpoint and makes full consecration, and who fully idealizes himself as great, and who makes every act, however trivial, an expression of the ideal, has already attained to greatness. Everything he does will be done in a great way. He will make himself known, and will be recognized as a personality of power. He will receive knowledge by inspiration, and will know all that he needs to know. He will receive all the material wealth he forms in his thoughts, and will not lack for any good thing. He will be given ability to deal with any combination of circumstances which may arise, and his growth and progress will be continuous and rapid. Great works will seek him out, and all men will delight to do him honor. Because of its peculiar value to the student of the Science of Being Great, I close this book by giving a portion of

Emerson's essay on the "Over soul." This great essay is fundamental, showing the foundation principles of monism and the science of greatness. I recommend the student to study it most carefully in connection with this book. What is the universal sense of want and ignorance, but the fine innuendo by which the great soul makes its enormous claim? Why do men feel that the natural history of man has never been written, but always he is leaving behind what you have said of him, and it becomes old, and books of metaphysics worthless? The philosophy of six thousand years has not searched the chambers and magazines of the soul. In its experiments there has always remained, in the last analysis, a residuum it could not resolve. Man is a stream whose source is hidden. Always our being is descending into us from we know not whence The most exact calculator has no prescience that somewhat incalculable may not balk the very next moment. I am constrained every moment to acknowledge a higher origin for events than the will I call mine. As with events, so it is with thoughts. When I watch that flowing river, which, out of regions I see not, pours for a season its streams into me, —I see that I am a pensioner, —not a cause, but a surprised spectator of this ethereal water; that I desire and look up, and put myself in the attitude for reception, but from some alien energy the visions come. Meantime within man is the soul of the whole; the wise silence; the universal beauty, to which every part and particle is equally related; the eternal One. And this deep power in which we exist, and whose beatitude is all accessible to us, is not only self sufficient and perfect in every hour, but the act of seeing, and the thing seen, the seer and the spectacle, the subject and the object, are one. We see the world piece by piece, as the sun, the moon, the animal, the tree; but the whole, of which these are the shining parts, is the soul. It is only by the vision of that Wisdom, that the horoscope of the ages can be read, and it is only by falling back on our better thoughts, by yielding to the spirit of prophecy which is innate in every man, that we know what it said. Every man's words, who speaks from that life, must sound vain to those who do not dwell in the same thought on their own part. I dare not speak for it. My words do not carry its august sense; they fall short and cold. Only itself can inspire whom it will, and behold! Their speech shall he lyrical and sweet, and universal as the rising of the wind. Yet I desire, even by profane words, if sacred I may not use, to indicate the heaven of this deity, and to report what hints I have collected of the transcendent simplicity and energy of the Highest Law. If we consider what happens in conversation, in reveries, in remorse, in times of passion, in surprises, in the instruction of dreams wherein often we see ourselves in masquerade, —the droll disguises only magnifying and enhancing a real element, and forcing it on our distinct notice, —we shall catch many hints that will broaden and lighten into knowledge of the secret of nature. All goes to show that the soul in man is not an organ, but animates and exercises all the organs; is not a function, like the power of memory, of calculation, of comparison, —but uses these as hands and feet; is not a faculty, but a light; is not the intellect or the will, but the master of the intellect and the will;— is the vast background of our being, in which they lie,— an immensity not possessed and that cannot be possessed. From within or from behind, a light shines through us upon things, and makes us aware that we are nothing, but the light is all. A man is the facade of a temple wherein all wisdom and all good abide. What we commonly call man, the eating, drinking, planting, counting man, does not, as we know him, represent himself, but misrepresents himself. Him we do not respect, but the soul, whose organ he is, would he let it appear through his action, would make our knees bend. When it breathes through his intellect, it is genius; when it flows through his affection it is love. After its own law and not by arithmetic is the rate of its progress to be computed. The soul's advances are not made by gradation, such as can be represented by motion in a straight line; but rather by ascension of state, such as can be represented by metamorphosis, —from the egg to the worm, from the worm to the fly. The growths of genius are of a certain total character, that does not advance the elect individual first over Adam, then Richard, and give to each the pain of discovered inferiority, but by every throe of growth the man expands there where he works, passing, at each pulsation, classes, populations of men. With each divine impulse the mind rends the thin rinds of the visible and finite, and comes out into eternity, and inspires and expires its air. It converses with truths that have always been spoken in the world, and becomes conscious of a closer sympathy with Zeno and Arrian, than with persons in the house. This is the law of moral and of mental gain. The simple rise as by specific levity, not into a particular virtue, but into the region of all the virtues. They are in the spirit which contains them all. The soul is superior to all the particulars of merit. The soul requires purity, but purity is not it; requires justice, but justice is not that; requires beneficence, but is somewhat better; so that there is a kind of descent and accommodation felt when we leave speaking of moral nature, to urge a virtue which it enjoins. For, to the soul in her pure action, all the virtues are natural, and not painfully acquired. Speak to his heart and the man becomes suddenly virtuous. Within the same sentiment is the germ of intellectual growth, which obeys the same law. Those who are capable of humility, of justice, of love, of aspiration, are already on a platform that commands the sciences and arts, speech and poetry, action and grace. For whoso dwells in this mortal beatitude, does already anticipate those special powers which men prize so highly; just as love does justice to all the gifts of the object beloved. The lover has no talent, no skill, which passes for quite nothing with his enamored maiden, however little she may possess of related faculty. And the heart which abandons itself to the God finds itself related to all its works and will travel a royal road to particular knowledge and powers. For, in ascending to this primary and aboriginal sentiment, we have come from our remote station on the circumference instantaneously to the center of the world, where, as in the closet of God, we see causes, and anticipate the universe, which is but a slow effect.

THE END

The Science of Being Well

By Wallace D. Wattles

Timeless wisdom and a practical program for vibrant health

www.bnpublishing.com

Table of Contents

Author's Preface

This volume is the second of a series, the first of which is The Science of Getting Rich. As that book is intended solely for those who want money, so this is for those who want health and a practical guide and handbook. This is not a philosophical treatise. It is an instructor in the use of the universal Principle of Life. My efforts have been to explain, in a plain and simple fashion that the reader, though he may not have any previous exposure to New Thought or metaphysics, may readily follow Wallace D. Wattles to perfect health. While retaining all essentials, I have carefully eliminated all non-essentials. I have not used any technical, abstruse, or difficult language, and have kept the one point in view at all times.

As the title asserts, this book deals with science, not speculation. The monistic theory of the universe — the theory that matter, mind, consciousness, and life are all manifestations of One Substance — is now accepted by most thinkers, and if you accept this theory, you cannot deny the logical conclusions you will find here. Best of all, the methods of thought and action prescribed have been tested by the author in his own case and in the case of hundreds of others during twelve years of practice, with continuous and unfailing success.

I can say of The Science of Being well that it works, and that wherever its laws are complied with, it can no more fail to work than the science of geometry can fail to work. If the tissues of your body have not been so destroyed that continued life is impossible, you can get well, and if you will think and act in a Certain Way, you will get well.

I would recommend the writings of Horace Fletcher and of Edward Hooker Dewey to those who wish more detailed information on the performance of the voluntary function of eating. Read these, if you like, as a sort of buttress to your faith, but let me warn you against making the mistake of studying many conflicting theories, and practicing, at the same time, parts of several different "systems." For if you get well, it must be by giving your WHOLE MIND to the right way of thinking and living.

Remember that The Science of Being Well claims to be a complete and sufficient guide in every way. Concentrate on both the way of thinking and acting it prescribes. Follow it in every detail and you will get well; or if you are already well, you will remain so.

Trusting that you will go on until the priceless blessing of perfect health is yours,
I remain,

Wallace D. Wattles

Chapter 1
The Principle of Health

In the personal application of The Science of Being Well, as in that of
The Science of Getting Rich, certain fundamental truths must be known in the
beginning and accepted without question. Some of these truths we state here:
The perfectly natural performance of function constitutes health, and the perfectly
natural performance of function results from the natural action of the Principle of
Life.

There is a Principle of Life in the universe, and it is the One Living Substance
from which all things are made. This Living Substance permeates, penetrates, and
fills the interspaces of the universe. It is in and through all things, like a very
refined and diffusible ether. All life comes from it — its life is all the life there is.

A human being is a form of this Living Substance and has within him a Principle
of Health. (The word Principle is used as meaning source.) The Prin-ciple of Health
in a person, when in full constructive activity, causes all the voluntary functions of
his life to be perfectly performed. It is the Principle of Health in a person which
really works all healing, no matter what "system" or "remedy" is employed, and this
Principle of Health is brought into Construc-tive Activity by thinking in a Certain
Way.

I proceed now to prove this last statement. We all know that cures are wrought
by all the different, and often opposite, methods employed in the various branches
of the healing art. The allopath, who gives a strong dose of a counter-poison, cures
his patient. And the homeopath, who gives a diminutive dose of the poison most
similar to that of the disease, also cures it. If allopathy ever cured any given disease,
it is certain that homeopathy never cured that disease. And if homeopathy ever
cured an ailment, allopathy could not possibly cure that ailment.* The two systems
are radically opposite in theory and practice, and yet both "cure" most diseases.
And even the remedies used by physicians in any one school are not the same.

Go with a case of indigestion to half a dozen doctors and compare their
prescriptions. It is more than likely that none of the ingredients of any one of them
will also be in the others. Must we not conclude that their patients are
healed by a Principle of Health within themselves, and not by something in the
varying "remedies"? Not only this, but we find the same ailments cured by the
osteopath with manipulations of the spine, by the faith healer with prayer, by the
food scientist with bills of fare, by the mental scientist with affirmation, and by the
hygienists with differing plans of living.

What conclusion can we come to in the face of all these facts but that there is a
Principle of Health which is the same in all people, and which really accomplishes
all the cures; and that there is something in all the "systems" which, under
favorable conditions, arouses the Principle of Health to action? That is, medicines,
manipulations, prayers, bills of fare, affirmations, and hygienic practices cure
whenever they cause the Principle of Health to become active, and fail whenever
they do not cause it to become active.

Does not all this indicate that the results depend upon the way the patient thinks about the remedy, rather than upon the ingredients in the prescription?

The Power that Heals is in the patient himself; whether it will become active or not does not depend upon the physical or mental means used, but upon the way the patient thinks about these means. There is a Universal Principle of Life— a great spiritual Healing Power — and there is a Principle of Health in every human being which is related to this Healing Power. This is dormant or active, according to the way a person thinks. He can always quicken it into activity by thinking in a Certain Way.

Your getting well does not depend upon the adoption of some system, or the finding of some remedy; people with your identical ailments have been healed by all systems and all remedies. It does not depend upon climate; some people are well and others are sick in all climates. It does not depend upon avocation, unless in case of those who work under poisonous conditions; people are well in all trades and professions. Your getting well depends upon your beginning to think — and act — in a Certain Way.

The way a person thinks about things is determined by what he believes about them. His thoughts are determined by his faith, and the results depend upon his making a personal application of his faith. If a person has faith in the efficacy of a medicine, and is able to apply that faith to himself, that medicine will certainly cause him to be cured. But though his faith be great, he will not be cured unless he applies it to himself. Many sick people have faith for others but none for themselves. So, if he has faith in a system of diet, and can personally apply that faith, it will cure him. And if he has faith in prayers and affirmations and personally applies his faith, prayers and affirmations will cure him.

Faith, personally applied, cures. And no matter how great the faith or how persistent the thought, it will not cure without personal application.

The Science of Being includes the two fields of thought and action. To be well it is not enough that a person should merely think in a Certain Way. He must apply his thought to himself, and he must express and externalize it in his outward life by acting in the same way that he thinks.

Chapter 2.
The Foundations of Faith

Before a person can think in the Certain Way which will cause his diseases to be healed, he must believe in certain truths: all things are made from one Living Substance, which, in its original state, permeates, penetrates, and fills the interspaces of the universe. While all visible things are made from It, yet this Substance — in its first formless condition — is in and through all the visible forms that It has made. Its life is in All and its intelligence is in All.

This Substance creates by thought, and its method is by taking the form of that which it thinks about. The thought of a form held by this substance causes it to assume that form; the thought of a motion causes it to institute that motion. Forms are created by this substance in moving itself into certain orientations or positions.

When original Substance wishes to create a given form, it thinks of the mo-tions which will produce that form. When it wishes to create a world, it thinks of the motions, perhaps extending through ages, which will result in its com-ing into the attitude and form of the world — and these motions are made. When it wishes to create an oak tree, it thinks of the sequences of movement, perhaps extending through ages, which will result in the form of an oak tree — and these motions are made. The particular sequences of motion by which differing forms should be produced were established in the beginning; they are changeless. Certain motions instituted in the Formless Substance will forever produce certain forms.

The human body is formed from the Original Substance, and is the result of certain motions, which first existed as thoughts of Original Substance. The mo-tions which produce, renew, and repair the body are called functions, and these functions are of two classes: voluntary and involuntary. The involuntary functions are under the control of the Principle of Health in a person, and are performed in a perfectly healthy manner so long as a person thinks in a certain way. The voluntary functions of life are eating, drinking, breathing, and sleeping. These, entirely or in part, are under the direction of a person's conscious mind, and he can perform them in a perfectly healthy way if he wills. If he does not perform them in a healthy way, he cannot remain well long. So we see that if a person thinks in a certain way, and eats, drinks, breathes, and sleeps in a corresponding way, he will be well.

The involuntary functions of a person's life are under the direct control of the Principle of Health, and so long as a person thinks in a perfectly healthy way, these functions are perfectly performed, for the action of the Principle of Health is largely directed by a person's conscious thought, affecting his subconscious mind.

A person is a thinking center, capable of originating thought, and as he does not know everything, he makes mistakes and thinks error. Not knowing everything, he believes things to be true which are not true. A person holds in his thought the idea of diseased and abnormal functioning and conditions, and so perverts the action of the Principle of Health, causing diseased and abnormal functioning and conditions within his own body.

The thoughts of perfect motion, perfect and healthy function, and complete life are held only in the Original Substance. God never thinks disease or imperfection.

But for countless ages people have held thoughts of disease, abnormality, old age, and death. And the perverted functioning resulting from these thoughts has become a part of the inheritance of the human race. Our ancestors have, for many generations, held imperfect ideas concerning human form and functioning, and we begin life with racial* sub-conscious impressions of im-perfection and disease. This is not natural, not a part of the plan of nature.

The purpose of nature can be nothing else than the perfection of life. This we see from the very nature of life itself. It is the nature of life to continually advance toward more perfect living; advancement is the inevitable result of the very act of living. Increase is always the result of active living; whatever lives must live more and more. The seed, lying in the granary, has life, but it is not living. Put it into the soil and it becomes active, and at once begins to gather to itself from the surrounding substance, and to build a plant form. It will cause such increase that a seed head will be produced containing 30, 60, or a hundred seeds, each having as much life as the first.

Life, by living, increases. Life cannot live without increasing, and the fundamental impulse of life is to live. It is in response to this fundamental impulse that Original Substance works, and creates. God must live, and God cannot live except as God creates and increases. In multiplying forms, God is moving on to live more.

The universe is a Great Advancing Life, and the purpose of nature is the advancement of life toward perfection, toward perfect functioning. The purpose of nature is perfect health.

The purpose of Nature, so far as a human being is concerned, is that he should be continuously advancing into more life, and progressing toward perfect life; and that he should live the most complete life possible in his present sphere of action.

*He is referring to "the human race" and to our collective consciousness, sometimes called "race thought."

This must be so, because that which lives in a person is seeking more life.
Give a little child a pencil and paper, and he begins to draw crude figures. That which lives in him is trying to express Itself in art. Give him a set of blocks, and he will try to build something. That which lives in him is seeking expression in architecture. Seat him at a piano, and he will try to draw harmony from the keys. That which lives in him is trying to express Itself in music. That which lives in a person is always seeking to live more, and since a person lives most when he is well, the Principle of Nature in him can seek only health. The natural state of a human being is a state of perfect health, and everything in him and in nature tends toward health.

Sickness can have no place in the thought of Original Substance, for it is by its own nature continually impelled toward the fullest and most perfect life — therefore, toward health. A human being, as he exists in the thought of the Formless Substance, has perfect health. Disease, which is abnormal or perverted function — motion imperfectly made, or made in the direction of imperfect life — has no place in the thought of the Thinking Stuff.

The Supreme Mind never thinks of disease. Disease was not created or ordained by God, or sent forth from God. It is wholly a product of separate consciousness, of the individual thought of a person. God, the Formless Substance, does not see disease, think disease, know disease, or recognize disease. Disease is recognized only by the thought of humanity; God thinks nothing but health.

From all the foregoing, we see that health is a fact or TRUTH in the Original Substance from which we are all formed, and that disease is an imperfect functioning resulting from the imperfect thoughts of people, past and present. If a person's thoughts of himself had always been those of perfect health, a person could not possibly now be otherwise than perfectly healthy.

A human being in perfect health is the thought of Original Substance, and a human being in imperfect health is the result of his own failure to think perfect health, and to perform the voluntary functions of life in a healthy way.

We will arrange a syllabus of The Science of Being Well basic truths. There is a Thinking Substance from which all things are made, and which, in its original state, permeates, penetrates, and fills the interspaces of the universe. It is the life of All. The thought of a form in this Substance causes the form; the thought of a motion produces the motion. In relation to humanity, the thoughts of this Substance are always of perfect functioning and perfect health. A person is a thinking center, capable of original thought; and his thought has power over his own functioning. By thinking imperfect thoughts he has caused imperfect and perverted functioning; and by performing the voluntary functions of life in a perverted manner, he has assisted in causing disease.

If a person will think only thoughts of perfect health, he can cause within himself the functioning of perfect health; all the Power of Life will be exerted to assist him. But this healthy functioning will not continue unless a person performs the external, or voluntary, functions of living in a healthy manner.

A person's first step must be to learn how to think perfect health; and his second step to learn how to eat, drink, breathe, and sleep in a perfectly healthy way. If a person takes these two steps, he will certainly become well, and remain so.

Chapter 3.
Life and Its Organisms

The human body is the abiding place of an energy which renews itself when worn, eliminates waste or poisonous matter, and repairs the body when broken or injured. This energy we call life. Life is not generated or produced within the body; it produces the body.

The seed which has been kept in the storehouse for years will grow when planted in the soil; it will produce a plant. But the life in the plant is not generated by its growing; it is the life which makes the plant grow.

The performance of function does not cause life; it is life which causes function to be performed. Life is first; function afterward.

It is life which distinguishes organic from inorganic matter, but it is not produced after the organization of matter. Life is the principle or force which causes organization; it builds organisms. It is a principle or force inherent in Original Substance; all life is One.

This Life Principle of the All is the Principle of Health in a person, and becomes constructively active whenever a person thinks in a Certain Way. Whoever, therefore, thinks in this Certain Way will surely have perfect health if his external functioning is in conformity with his thought. But the external functioning must conform to the thought; a person cannot hope to be well by thinking health if he eats, drinks, breathes, and sleeps like a sick person.

The universal Life Principle, then, is the Principle of Health in a human be-ing. It is one with original substance. There is one Original Substance from which all things are made; this substance is alive, and its life is the Principle of Life of the universe. This Substance has created from itself all the forms of or-ganic life by thinking them, or by thinking the motions and functions which produce them. Original Substance thinks only health, because It knows all truth. There is no truth which is not known in the Formless, which is All, and in all. It not only knows all truth, but it has all power. Its vital power is the source of all the energy there is. A conscious life which knows all truth and which has all power cannot go wrong or perform function imperfectly. Knowing all, it knows too much to go wrong, and so the Formless cannot be diseased or think disease.

A human being is a form of this Original Substance and has a separate consciousness of his own; but his consciousness is limited, and therefore imperfect. By reason of his limited knowledge a person can and does think wrongly, and so he causes perverted and imperfect functioning in his own body. A human being has not yet known enough not to go wrong. The diseased or imperfect functioning may not instantly result from an imperfect thought, but it is bound to come if the thought becomes habitual. Any thought continuously held by a person tends to the establishment of the corresponding condition in his body.

Also, the human being has failed to learn how to perform the voluntary functions of his life in a healthy way. He does not know when, what, and how to eat. He knows little about breathing and less about sleep. He does all these things in a wrong way, and under wrong conditions. And this because he has neglected to follow the only sure guide to the knowledge of life. He has tried to live by logic rather than by instinct. He has made living a matter of art, and not of nature. And he has gone wrong.

His only remedy is to begin to go right, and this he can surely do. It is the focus of this book to teach the whole truth, so that the person who reads it shall know too much to go wrong.

The thoughts of disease produce the forms of disease. A person must learn to think health; and being Original Substance which takes the form of its thoughts, he will become the form of health and manifest perfect health in all his functioning. The people who were healed by the doses of either the allopath or the homeopath were also really healed by thinking in a Certain Way; there is no drug which has within itself the power to heal disease.

The people who have been healed by prayers and affirmations were also healed by thinking in a certain way; there is no curative power in strings of words. All the sick who have been healed, by whatsoever "system," have thought in a Certain Way; and a little examination will show us what this way is.

The two essentials of the Way are Faith and a Personal Application of the Faith. These are the two essentials to thinking in the Certain Way which will make you well: first, claim or appropriate health by faith, and, second, sever all mental relations with disease and enter into mental relations with health.

That which we make ourselves, mentally, we become physically, and that with which we unite ourselves mentally we become unified with physically. If your thought always relates you to disease, then your thought becomes a fixed power to cause disease within you. And if your thought always relates you to health, then your thought becomes a fixed power exerted to keep you well.

In the case of the people who are healed by medicines, the result is obtained in the same way. They have, consciously or unconsciously, sufficient faith in the means used that they sever mental relations with disease and enter into mental relations with health.

Faith may be unconscious. It is possible for us to have a subconscious or inbred faith in things like medicine; in which we do not believe to any extent objectively, and this subconscious faith may be quite sufficient to quicken the Principle of Health into constructive activity. Many who have little conscious faith are healed in this way, while many others who have great faith in the means are not healed because they do not make the personal application to themselves. Their faith is general, but not specific for their own cases.

In the Science of Being Well we have two main points to consider: first, how to think with faith, and, second, how to so apply the thought to ourselves as to quicken the Principle of Health into constructive activity.

We begin by learning What to Think.

Chapter 4.
What To Think

In order to sever all mental relations with disease, you must first enter into mental relations with health, making the process positive, not negative — one of assumption, not of rejection. You are to receive or appropriate health rather than to reject and deny disease. Denying disease accomplishes next to nothing. When you enter into full and constant mental relations with health, out of necessity you must cease all relationship with disease.

The first step in the Science of Being Well, then, is to enter into complete thought connection with health. The best way to do this is to form a mental image or picture of yourself as being well, imagining a perfectly strong and healthy body, and to spend sufficient time in contemplating this image to make it your habitual thought of yourself.

This is not so easy as it sounds. It necessitates the taking of considerable time for meditation, and not all persons have the imaging faculty well enough developed to form a distinct mental picture of themselves in a perfect or idealized body. It is much easier, as in The Science of Getting Rich, to form a mental image of the things one wants to have as we have seen these things or their counterparts and know how they look. We can picture them very easily from memory. But if we have never seen ourselves in a perfect body, a clear mental image is hard to form.

It is not necessary or essential, however, to have a clear mental image of yourself as you wish to be; it is only essential to form a CONCEPTION of perfect health and to relate yourself to it. This Conception of Health is not a mental picture of a particular thing. It is an understanding of health and carries with it the idea of perfect functioning in every part and organ. You may TRY to picture yourself as perfect in physique — that helps — and you MUST think of yourself as doing everything in the manner of a perfectly strong and healthy person.

You can picture yourself as walking down the street with an erect body and a vigorous stride. You can picture yourself as doing your day's work easily and with surplus vigor, never tired or weak. You can picture in your mind how all things would be done by a person full of health and power, and you can make yourself the central figure in the picture, doing things in just that way. Never think of the ways in which weak or sickly people do things; always think of the way strong people do things. Spend your leisure time in thinking about the Strong Way, until you have a good conception of it, and always think of yourself in connection with the Strong Way of Doing Things. That is what I mean by having a Conception of Health.

In order to establish perfect functioning in every part, a person does not have to study anatomy or physiology so that he can form a mental image of each separate organ and address himself to it. He does not have to "treat" his liver, his kidneys, his stomach, or his heart. There is one Principle of Health in a human being which has control over all the involuntary functions of his life. And the thought of perfect health, impressed upon by this Principle, will reach each part and organ. A person's liver is not controlled by a liver principle, his stomach by a digestive principle, and so on. The Principle of Health is One.

The less you go into the detailed study of physiology, the better for you. Our knowledge of this science is very imperfect and leads to imperfect thought. Imperfect thought causes imperfect functioning, which is disease.

Let me illustrate: Until quite recently, physiology fixed ten days as the ex-treme limit of a human being's endurance without food. It was considered that only in exceptional cases could a person survive a longer fast. So the impres-sion became universally disseminated that one who was deprived of food must die within five to ten days. And numbers of people, when cut off from food by shipwreck, accident, or famine, did die within this period.

But the performances of Dr. Tanner, the 40-day faster, and the writings of Dr. Dewey and others on the fasting cure, together with the experiments of numberless people who have fasted from 40 to 60 days, have shown that a human's ability to live without food is vastly greater than had been previously supposed.

Any person, properly educated, can fast from 20 to 40 days with little loss in weight, and often with no apparent loss of strength at all. The people who starved to death in ten days or less did so because they believed that death was inevitable. An erroneous physiology had given them a wrong thought about themselves. When a person is deprived of food he will die within 10 to 50 days, according to the way he has been taught, or, in other words, according to the way he thinks about it. So you see that an erroneous physiology can work very mischievous results.

No Science of Being Well can be founded on current physiology; it is not sufficiently exact in its knowledge. With all its pretensions, comparatively little is really known as to the interior workings and processes of the body. It is not known just how food is digested. It is not known just what part food plays, if any, in the generation of force. It is not known exactly what the liver, spleen, and pancreas are for, or what part their secretions play in the chemistry of assimilation. On all these and most other points we theorize, but we do not really know.

When a person begins to study physiology, he enters the domain of theory and disputation. He comes among conflicting opinions, and he is bound to form mistaken ideas. These mistaken ideas lead to the thinking of wrong thoughts and this leads to perverted functioning and disease. All that the most perfect knowledge of physiology could do for a person would be to enable him to think only thoughts of perfect health, and to eat, drink, breathe, and sleep in a perfectly healthy way. And this, as we shall show, he can do without studying physiology at all. This, for the most part, is true of all hygiene. There are certain fundamental propositions which we should know, and these will be explained in later chapters, but aside from these propositions, ignore physiology and hygiene. They tend to fill your mind with thoughts of imperfect conditions, and these thoughts will produce the imperfect conditions in your own body.

You cannot study any "science" which recognizes disease, if you are to think nothing but health. Drop all investigation as to your present condition, its causes, or possible results, and set yourself to the work of forming a conception of health. Think about health and the possibilities of health; of the work that may be done and the pleasures that may be enjoyed in a condition of perfect health. Then make this conception your guide in thinking of yourself. Refuse to entertain for an instant any thought of yourself which is not in harmony with it. When any idea of disease or imperfect functioning enters your mind, cast it out instantly by calling up a thought which is in harmony with the Conception of Health.

Think of yourself at all times as realizing this conception, as being a strong and perfectly healthy personage, and do not harbor a contrary thought.
KNOW that as you think of yourself in unity with this conception, the Original Substance which permeates and fills the tissues of your body is taking form according to the thought. Know that this Intelligent Substance or mind stuff will cause function to be performed in such a way that your body will be rebuilt with perfectly healthy cells.

The Intelligent Substance, from which all things are made, permeates and penetrates all things; and so it is in and through your body. It moves according to its thoughts, and so if you hold only the thoughts of perfectly healthy function, it will cause the movements of perfectly healthy function within you.
Hold with persistence to the thought of perfect health in relation to yourself. Do not permit yourself to think in any other way. Hold this thought with per-fect faith that it is the fact, the truth. It is the truth so far as your mental body is concerned.

You have a mind-body and a physical body. The mind-body takes form just as you think of yourself, and any thought which you hold continuously is made visible by the transformation of the physical body into its image. Implanting the thought of perfect functioning in the mind-body will, in due time, cause perfect functioning in the physical body.

The transformation of the physical body into the image of the ideal held by the mind-body is not accomplished instantaneously. In the creation and recreation of forms, Substance moves along the fixed lines of growth it has established, and the impression upon it of the health thought causes the healthy body to be built cell by cell. Holding only thoughts of perfect health will ultimately cause perfect functioning, and perfect functioning will in due time produce a perfectly healthy body.

It may be well to condense this chapter into a syllabus: Your physical body is permeated and filled with an Intelligent Substance, which forms a body of mind-stuff. This mind-stuff controls the functioning of your physical body. A thought of disease or of imperfect function, impressed upon the mind-stuff, causes disease or imperfect functioning in the physical body. If you are diseased, it is because wrong thoughts have made impressions on this mind-stuff. These may have been either your own thoughts or those of your parents — we begin life with many subconscious impressions, both right and wrong. But the natural tendency of all minds is toward health, and if no thoughts are held in the conscious mind save those of health, all internal functioning will come to be performed in a perfectly healthy manner.

The Power of Nature within you is sufficient to overcome all hereditary impressions. If you will learn to control your thoughts, so that you will think only those of health, and if you will perform the voluntary functions of life in a perfectly healthy way, you can certainly be well.

Editor's Note:
In 1910, very little was known about physiology and pathology — the inner workings of the body in health and disease. Today, almost a century later, de-spite

huge advances in medical science, the human body is still largely a mys-tery. The process of mapping the intricate genetic code that makes us human (the "Human Genome Project") has called into question what every present-day doctor was taught in school about the most basic function in our cells — the role of DNA. The implications of this are at least as dramatic as the discovery that the earth is not flat!

Amazingly enough, cutting-edge science supports exactly what Mr. Wattles wrote in this last paragraph, which bears repeating: the Power of Nature within you is sufficient to overcome all hereditary impressions, and if you will learn to control your thoughts, so that you will think only those of health, and if you will perform the voluntary functions of life in a perfectly healthy way, you can certainly be well.

Chapter 5.
Faith

The Principle of Health is moved by Faith. Nothing else can call it into action, Only faith can enable you to relate yourself to health and sever your relation with disease in your thoughts. You will continue to think of disease unless you have faith in health. If you do not have faith, you will doubt. If you doubt, you will fear. And if you fear, you will relate yourself in mind to that which you fear.

If you fear disease, you will think of yourself in connection with disease, and that will produce within yourself the form and motions of disease. Just as Original Substance creates from itself the forms of its thoughts, so your mind-body, which is original substance, takes the form and motion of whatever you think about. If you fear disease, dread disease, have doubts about your safety from disease, or if you even contemplate disease, you will connect yourself with it and create its forms and motions within you.

Let me enlarge somewhat upon this point. The potency, or creative power, of a thought is given to it by the faith that is in it. Thoughts which contain no faith create no forms. The Formless Substance, which knows all truth and therefore thinks only truth, has perfect faith in every thought, because it thinks only truth, and so all its thoughts create. But if you will imagine a thought in Formless Substance in which there was no faith, you will see that such a thought could not cause the Substance to move or take form. Keep in mind the fact that only those thoughts which are conceived in faith have creative energy. Only those thoughts which have faith with them are able to change function, or to quicken the Principle of Health into activity.

If you do not have faith in health, you will certainly have faith in disease. If you do not have faith in health, it will do you no good to think about health, for your thoughts will have no potency, and will cause no change for the better in your conditions. If you do not have faith in health, I repeat, you will have faith in disease. And if, under such conditions, you think about health for ten hours a day and think about disease for only a few minutes, the disease thought will control your condition because it will have the potency of faith, while the health thought will not. Your mind-body will take on the form and motions of disease and retain them, because your health thought will not have sufficient dynamic force to change form or motion.

In order to practice the Science of Being Well, you must have complete faith in health. Faith begins in belief; and we now come to the question: What must you believe in order to have faith in health?

You must believe that there is more health-power than disease-power in both yourself and your environment; and you cannot help believing this if you consider the facts. These are the facts: There is a Thinking Substance from which all things are made, and which, in its original state, permeates, penetrates, and fills the interspaces of the universe. The thought of a form, in this Substance, produces the form; the thought of a motion institutes the motion. In relation to the human being, the thoughts of Original Substance are always of perfect health and perfect functioning. This Substance, within and without a human being, always exerts its power toward health.

A person is a thinking center, capable of original thought. He has a mind-body of Original Substance permeating a physical body, and the functioning of his physical body is determined by the FAITH of his mind-body. If a person thinks with faith of the functioning of health, he will cause his internal functions to perform in a healthy manner, provided that he performs the ex-ternal functions in a corresponding manner. But if a person thinks, with faith, of disease, or of the power of disease, he will cause his internal functioning to be the functioning of disease.

The Original Intelligent Substance is in a human being, moving toward health — and it is pressing upon him from every side. The human being lives, moves, and has his being in a limitless ocean of health-power, and he uses this power according to his faith. If he appropriates it and applies it to himself it is all his, and if he unifies himself with it by unquestioning faith, he cannot fail to attain health, for the power of this Substance is all the power there is.

A belief in the above statements is a foundation for faith in health. If you believe them, you believe that health is the natural state of humanity, and that a human being lives in the midst of Universal Health — that all the power of nature makes for health, and that health is possible to all, and can surely be attained by all. You will believe that the power of health in the universe is 10,000 times greater than that of disease — in fact, that disease has no power whatever, being only the result of perverted thought and faith. And if you believe that health is possible to you, and that it may surely be attained by you, and that you know exactly what to do in order to attain it, you will have faith in health. You will have this faith and knowledge if you read this book through with care and determination to believe in and practice its teachings.

It is not merely the possession of faith, but the personal application of faith which works healing. You must claim health in the beginning, and form a conception of health, and, as far as may be, of yourself as a perfectly healthy person. And then, by faith, you must claim that you ARE REALIZING this conception.

Do not assert with faith that you are going to get well; assert with faith that you ARE well. Having faith in health, and applying it to yourself, means hav-ing faith that you are healthy. And the first step in this is to claim that it is the truth.

Mentally take the attitude of being well, and do not say anything or do anything which contradicts this attitude. Never speak a word or assume a physical attitude which does not harmonize with the claim: "I am perfectly well." When you walk, go with a brisk step, and with your chest thrown out and your head held up. Watch that at all times your physical actions and attitudes are those of a healthy person. When you find that you have relapsed into the attitude of weakness or disease, change instantly: straighten up, and think of health and power. Refuse to consider yourself as other than a perfectly healthy person.

One great aid — perhaps the greatest aid — in applying your faith you will find in the exercise of gratitude. Whenever you think of yourself, or of your advancing condition, give thanks to the God for the perfect health you are enjoying. Remember that there is a continual inflow of life from God, which is received by all created things according to their forms. Health from God is continually being urged upon you, and when you think of this, lift up your mind, and give thanks of perfect health of mind and body. Be, all the time, in a grateful frame of mind, and let gratitude be evident in your speech. Gratitude will help you to own and control your own field of thought.

Whenever the thought of disease is presented to you, instantly claim health, and thank God for the perfect health you have. Do this so that there will be no room in your mind for a thought of ill. Every thought connected in any way with ill health is unwelcome, and you can close the door of your mind in its face by asserting that you are well, and by thanking God that it is so. Soon the old thoughts will return no more.

Gratitude has a twofold effect: it strengthens your own faith and you relate yourself closer to God by feeling continuous gratitude. It is plain, then, that the person who feels deep and hearty gratitude will live in closer touch with God than the person who never looks to God in thankfulness. The ungrateful or unthankful mind really denies that it receives at all, and so cuts its connection with God. The grateful mind is always looking toward God.

The Principle of Health in a human being receives its vital power from the Principle of Life in the universe, and a person relates himself to the Principle of Life by faith in health, and by gratitude for the health he receives.

A person may cultivate both faith and gratitude by the proper use of his will.

Chapter 6.
Use of the Will

In the practice of the Science of Being Well, the will is not used to compel yourself to go when you are not really able to go or to do things when you are not physically strong enough to do them. You do not direct your will upon your physical body or try to compel the proper performance of internal function by will power.

You direct the will upon the mind, and use it in determining what you shall believe, what you shall think, and to what you shall give your attention. The will should never be used upon any person or thing external to you, and it should never be used upon your own body. The sole legitimate use of the will is in determining to what you shall give your attention and what you shall think about the things to which your attention is given.

All belief begins in the will to believe. You cannot always and instantly believe what you will to believe; but you can always will to believe what you want to believe. You want to believe truth about health, and you can will to do so. The statements you have been reading in this book are the truth about health, and you can will to believe them. This must be your first step toward getting well.

This is the statement you must will to believe: That if a person will think only thoughts of perfect health, he must and will cause the internal and involuntary functioning of his body to be the functioning of health, provided that his external and voluntary functioning and attitude are in accordance with his thoughts. When you will to believe this statement, you must also begin to act upon it. You cannot retain a belief long unless you act upon it, you cannot increase a belief until it becomes faith unless you act upon it, and you certainly cannot expect to reap benefits in any way from a belief so long as you act as if the opposite were true. You cannot long have faith in health if you continue to act like a sick person. If you continue to act like a sick person, you cannot help continuing to think of yourself as a sick person. And if you continue to think of yourself as a sick person, you will continue to be a sick person.

The first step toward acting externally like a well person is to begin to act internally like a well person. Form your conception of perfect health and get into the way of thinking about perfect health until it begins to have a definite meaning to you. Picture yourself as doing the things a strong and healthy person would do; have faith that you can and will do those things in that way. Continue this until you have a vivid CONCEPTION of health and what it means to you.

When I speak in this book of a conception of health, I mean a conception that carries with it the idea of the way a healthy person looks and does things. Think of yourself in connection with health until you form a conception of how you would live, appear, act, and do things as a perfectly healthy person. Think about yourself in connection with health until you conceive of yourself, in imagination, as always doing everything in the manner of a well person — until the thought of health conveys the idea of what health means to you. As I have said in a former chapter, you may not be able to form a clear mental image of yourself in perfect health, but you can form a conception of yourself as acting like a healthy person.

Form this conception, and then think only thoughts of perfect health in relation to yourself, and so far as may be possible, in relation to others. When a thought of sickness or disease is presented to you, reject it. Do not let it get into your mind. Do not entertain or consider it at all. Meet it by thinking health, by thinking that you are well, and by being sincerely grateful for the health you are receiving.

Whenever suggestions of disease are coming thick and fast upon you, and you are in a "tight place," fall back upon the exercise of gratitude. Connect yourself with God, giving thanks for the perfect health God gives you, and you will soon find yourself able to control your thoughts, and to think what you want to think. In times of doubt, trial, and temptation, the exercise of gratitude is always a sheet anchor which will prevent you from being swept away.

Remember that the great essential thing is to SEVER ALL MENTAL RELATIONS WITH DISEASE AND TO ENTER INTO FULL MENTAL RELATIONSHIP WITH HEALTH. This is the KEY to all mental healing; it is the whole thing.

Exercise your will power in choosing only those thoughts which are thoughts of health, and arrange your environment so that it will suggest thoughts of health. Do not have about you books, pictures, or other things which suggest death, disease, deformity, weakness, or age. Have only those which convey the ideas of health, power, joy, vitality, and youth. When you are confronted with a book, or anything else which suggests disease, do not give it your attention.

Think of your conception of health, and your gratitude, and affirm as above. Use your will power to fix your attention upon thoughts of health. In a future chapter I shall touch upon this point again. What I wish to make plain here is that you must think only health, recognize only health, and give your attention only to health, and that you must control thought, recognition, and attention by the use of your will.

Everything in the universe wants you to be well. You have absolutely nothing to overcome but your own habit of thinking in a certain way about disease, and you can do this only by forming a habit of thinking in another Certain Way about health.

A person can cause all the internal functions of his body to be performed in a perfectly healthy manner by continuously thinking in a Certain Way and by performing the external functions in a certain way. He can think in this Certain Way by controlling his attention, and he can control his attention by the use of his will. He can decide what things he will think about.

Chapter 7.
Health from God

I will give a chapter here to explain how a human being may receive health from G-d who is the source of all energy and power, and constitutes the "inflow" of life, vitalizing all things.

With wisdom comes poise, and the power to think rightly, to control and guide your thoughts, and to avoid the difficulties which come from wrong thinking. With wisdom you will be able to select the right courses for your particular needs, and to so govern yourself in all ways as to secure the best results. You will know how to do what you want to do. You can readily see that wisdom must be an essential attribute of God, since God knows all truth.

A person can live in three general ways: for the gratification of his body, for that of his intellect, or for that of his soul. The first is accomplished by satisfying the desires for food, drink, and those other things which give enjoyable physical sensations. The second is accomplished by doing those things which cause pleasant mental sensations, such as gratifying the desire for knowledge or those for fine clothing, fame, power, and so on. The third is accomplished by giving way to the instincts of unselfish love and altruism.

A person lives most wisely and completely when he functions most perfectly along all of these lines, without excess in any of them. The person who lives swinishly, for the body alone, is unwise and out of harmony with God. That person who lives solely for the cold enjoyments of the intellect, though he be absolutely moral, is unwise and out of harmony with God. And the person who lives wholly for the practice of altruism, and who throws himself away for others, is as unwise and as far from harmony with God as those who go to excess in other ways.

To come into full harmony with God, you must purpose to LIVE — to live to the utmost of your capabilities in body, mind, and soul.. This must mean the full exercise of function in all the different ways, but without excess, for excess in one causes deficiency in the others. Behind your desire for health is your own desire for more abundant life. So, as you advance toward perfect health, hold steadily to the purpose to attain complete life, physical, mental, and spiritual; to advance in all ways, and in every way walking faithfully and humbly in God's ways.

Professor James* has pointed out that there is apparently no limit to the powers of the human being, and this is simply because the human being's power comes from God's inexhaustible reservoir. The runner who has reached the stage of exhaustion, when his physical power seems entirely gone, by running on in a Certain Way may receive his "second wind." His strength is renewed in a seemingly miraculous fashion, and he can go on indefinitely. And by continuing in the Certain Way, he may receive a third, fourth, and fifth "wind." We do not know where the limit is, or how far it may be possible to extend it.

The conditions are that the runner must have absolute faith that the strength will come, that he must think steadily of strength and have perfect confidence that he has it, and that he must continue to run on. If he admits a doubt into his mind, he falls exhausted, and if he stops running to wait for the accession of strength, it will never come. His faith in strength, his faith that he can keep on running, his unwavering purpose** to keep on running, and his action in keeping on seem to connect him to the source of energy in such a way as to bring him a new supply.

In a very similar manner, the sick person who has unquestioning faith in health, whose purpose brings him into harmony with God, and who performs the voluntary functions of life in a certain way, will receive vital energy sufficient for all his needs, and for the healing of all his diseases.

God, who seeks to live and express himself fully in humanity, delights to give human beings all that is needed for the most abundant life.

*William James, MD (1842-1910), sometimes called "the father of modern psychology."

**Mr. Wattles often uses the word purpose in its old-fashioned meaning: determination. He also usesit as a verb, to purpose: to be determined or committed, as in, "He purposed to succeed."

Chapter 8.
Summary of the Mental Actions

Let me now summarize the mental actions and attitudes necessary to the practice of the Science of Being Well: first, you believe that God is a Thinking Substance, from which all things are made, and which, in its original state, permeates, penetrates, and fills the interspaces of the universe. This Substance is the Life of All, and is seeking to express more life in all. It is the Principle of Life of the universe, and the Principle of Health in a human being.

A human being draws his vitality from it. He is a mind-body of original substance, permeating a physical body, and the thoughts of his mind-body control the functioning of his physical body. If a person thinks no thoughts save those of perfect health, the functions of his physical body will be performed in a manner of perfect health.

In order to consciously relate yourself to the All-Health, your purpose must be to live fully on every plane of your being. You must want all that there is in life for body, mind, and soul, and this will bring you into harmony with all the life there is.

The person who is in conscious and intelligent harmony with All will receive a continuous inflow of vital power from God, and this inflow is prevented by angry, selfish or antagonistic mental attitudes. If you are against any part, you have severed relations with all — you will receive life, but only instinctively and automatically, not intelligently and purposefully. You can see that if you are mentally antagonistic to any part, you cannot be in complete harmony with the Whole.. The reader is recommended to read what we have said in a former work (The Science of Getting Rich) concerning the Competitive mind and the Creative mind. It is very doubtful whether one who has lost health can completely regain it so long as he remains in the competitive mind.

Being on the Creative or Good-Will plane in mind, the next step is to form a conception of yourself as in perfect health, and to hold no thoughts which are not in full harmony with this conception. Have FAITH that if you think only thoughts of health you will establish in your physical body the functioning of health; and use your will to determine that you will think only thoughts of health.

Never think of yourself as sick, or as likely to be sick; never think of sickness in connection with yourself at all. And, as far as may be, shut out of your mind all thoughts of sickness in connection with others. Surround yourself as much as possible with the things which suggest the ideas of strength and health.

Have faith in health, and accept health as an actual present fact in your life. Claim health as a blessing bestowed upon you by God and be deeply grateful at all times. Claim the blessing by faith, know that it is yours, and never admit a contrary thought to your mind.

Use your will-power to withhold your attention from every appearance of disease in yourself and others. Do not study disease, think about it, nor speak of it. At all times, when the thought of disease is thrust upon you, move forward into the mental position of prayerful gratitude for your perfect health.

The mental actions necessary to being well may now be summed up in a single sentence: Form a conception of yourself in perfect health, and think only those thoughts which are in harmony with that conception. That — with faith and gratitude and the purpose to really live — covers all the requirements.

It is not necessary to take mental exercises of any kind, except as described in Chapter 6, or to do wearying "stunts" in the way of affirmations, and so on. It is not necessary to concentrate the mind on the affected parts. It is far better not to think of any part as affected. It is not necessary to "treat" yourself by auto-suggestion, or to have others treat you in any way whatever. The power that heals is the Principle of Health within you, and to call this Principle into Constructive Action it is only necessary, having harmonized yourself with the All-Mind, to claim by FAITH the All-Health and to hold that claim until it is physically manifested in all the functions of your body.

In order to hold this mental attitude of faith, gratitude, and health, however, your external acts must be only those of health. You cannot sustain the internal attitude of a well person if you continue to perform the external acts of a sick person. It is essential not only that your every thought should be a thought of health, but that your every act should be an act of health, performed in a healthy manner. If you will make every thought a thought of health, and every conscious act an act of health, it must infallibly follow that every internal and unconscious function shall come to be healthy, for all the power of life is being continually exerted toward health.

We shall next consider how you may make every act an act of health.

Chapter 9.
When To Eat

You cannot build and maintain a perfectly healthy body by mental action alone, or by the performance of the unconscious or involuntary functions alone. There are certain actions, more or less voluntary, which have a direct and immediate relation with the continuance of life itself. These are eating, drinking, breathing, and sleeping.

No matter what a person's thought or mental attitude may be, he cannot live unless he eats, drinks, breathes, and sleeps. Moreover, he cannot be well if he eats, drinks, breathes, and sleeps in an unnatural or wrong manner. It is therefore vitally important that you should learn the right way to perform these voluntary functions. I shall proceed to show you this way, beginning with the matter of eating, which is most important.

There has been a vast amount of controversy as to when to eat, what to eat, how to eat, and how much to eat. All this controversy is unnecessary, for the Right Way is very easy to find. You have only to consider the Law which governs all attainment, whether of health, wealth, power, or happiness; and that law is that you must do what you can do now, where you are now; do every separate act in the most perfect manner possible, by putting the power of faith into every action.

The processes of digestion and assimilation are under the supervision and control of an inner division of a person's mentality, which is generally called the subconscious mind. I shall use this term here in order to be understood. The subconscious mind is in charge of all the functions and processes of life, and when more food is needed by the body, it makes the fact known by causing a sensation called hunger.

Whenever food is needed and can be used, there is hunger, and whenever there is hunger it is time to eat. When there is no hunger it is unnatural and wrong to eat, no matter how great may APPEAR to be the need for food.

Even if you are in a condition of apparent starvation, with great emaciation, if there is no hunger you may know that FOOD CANNOT BE USED, and it will be unnatural and wrong for you to eat.*

*See the section "Is Prolonged Fasting Safe?" in the Editor's Notes at the end of this chapter.

Though you have not eaten for days or weeks, if you have no hunger you may be perfectly sure that food cannot be used, and will probably not be used if taken. Whenever food is needed, if there is power to digest and assimilate it, so that it can be normally used, the subconscious mind will announce the fact by a decided hunger.

Food, taken when there is no hunger, will sometimes be digested and assimilated, because nature makes a special effort to perform the task which is thrust upon her against her will. But if food is habitually taken when there is no hunger, the digestive power is at last destroyed, and numberless evils caused.

If the foregoing be true — and it is indisputably so — it is a self-evident proposition that the natural time (and the healthy time) to eat is when one is hungry, and that it is never a natural or a healthy action to eat when one is not hungry. You see, then, that it is an easy matter to scientifically settle the ques-tion when to eat. ALWAYS eat when you are hungry, and NEVER eat when you are not hungry. This is obedience to nature, which is obedience to God.

We must not fail, however, to make clear the distinction between hunger and appetite. Hunger is the call of the subconscious mind for more material to be used in repairing and renewing the body, and in keeping up the internal heat. Hunger is never felt unless there is need for more material, and unless there is power to digest it when taken into the stomach. Appetite is a desire for the gratification of sensation. The drunkard has an appetite for liquor, but he cannot have a hunger for it. A normally fed person cannot have a hunger for candy or sweets. The desire for these things is an appetite. You cannot hunger for tea, coffee, spiced foods, or for the various taste-tempting devices of the skilled cook. If you desire these things, it is with appetite, not with hunger.

Hunger is nature's call for material to be used in building new cells, and nature never calls for anything which may not be legitimately used for this purpose. Appetite is often largely a matter of habit. If one eats or drinks at a certain hour, and especially if one takes sweetened or spiced and stimulating foods, the desire comes regularly at the same hour, but this habitual desire for food should never be mistaken for hunger. Hunger does not appear at specified times. It only comes when work or exercise has used sufficient energy to make the taking in of new raw material a necessity. For instance, if a person has been sufficiently fed on the preceding day, it is impossible that he should feel a genuine hunger on arising from refreshing sleep. In sleep the body is recharged with vital power, and the assimilation of the food which has been taken during the day is completed — the system has no need for food immediately after sleep, unless the person went to his rest in a state of starvation. With a system of feeding which is even a reasonable approach to a natural one, no one can have a real hunger for an early morning breakfast. There is no such thing possible as a normal or genuine hunger immediately after arising from sound sleep.

The early morning breakfast is always taken to gratify appetite, never to satisfy hunger. No matter who you are, or what your condition is; no matter how hard you work, or how much you are exposed, unless you go to your bed starved, you cannot arise from your bed hungry.

Hunger is not caused by sleep, but by work. And it does not matter who you are, or what your condition, or how hard or easy your work, the so-called
no-breakfast plan is the right plan for you. It is the right plan for everybody, because it is based on the universal law that hunger never comes until it is EARNED. I am aware that a protest against this will come from the large number of people who "enjoy" their breakfasts, whose breakfast is their "best meal," who believe that their work is so hard that they cannot "get through the before-noon on an empty stomach, "and so on. But all their arguments fall down before the facts.

They enjoy their breakfast as the toper enjoys his morning dram, because it gratifies a habitual appetite and not because it supplies a natural want. It is their best meal for the same reason that his morning dram is the toper's best drink. And they CAN get along without it, because millions of people, of every trade and profession, DO get along without it, and are vastly better for doing so. If you are to live according to the Science of Being Well, you must NEVER EAT UNTIL YOU

HAVE AN EARNED HUNGER. But if I do not eat on arising in the morning, when shall I take my first meal?

In 99 cases out of a hundred twelve o'clock noon is early enough, and it is generally the most convenient time. If you are doing heavy work, you will get by noon a hunger sufficient to justify a good-sized meal. And if your work is light, you will probably still have hunger enough for a moderate meal. The best general rule or law that can be laid down is that you should eat your first meal of the day at noon if you are hungry, and if you are not hungry, wait until you become so.

And when shall I eat my second meal?

Not at all, unless you are hungry for it — and that with a genuine earned hunger. If you do get hungry for a second meal, eat at the most convenient time, but do not eat until you have a really earned hunger. The reader who wishes to fully inform himself as to the reasons for this way of arranging the mealtimes will find the best books thereon cited in the preface to this work. From the foregoing, however, you can easily see that The Science of Being Well readily answers the question, when, and how often shall I eat?

The answer: Eat when you have an earned hunger, and never eat at any other time.

Editor's Notes

In 1910, before the discovery of vitamins or calories, the role of food for life and health was unclear to most of western, white society. Even among western medical doctors, the process of digestion within the stomach and intestines was not yet understood. The roles of the liver, gall bladder, and pancreas were not known. How food was absorbed and transported throughout the body was unknown. The actual cellular processes of the human body were an utter mystery.

Mr. Wattles reasoned that work, whether mental or physical, "used up" or destroyed cells which must then be replaced. Hunger was the body's signal that cells needed to be built. Sleep, however, was fully restorative, required no work, and resulted in increased energy. Therefore, he reasoned, sleep could not result in hunger, because it used no cells.

Is the 'No-Breakfast Plan' the One for You?

First, understand that because your body does most of its growing and repair work during the night while you are sleeping, it is physiologically possible for you to generate some hunger. But it is rarely enough to require food immedi-ately on rising. The body's requirements during sleep are generally filled by the food eaten at previus meals is still being absorbed from the digestive tract.

Most people who experiment with fasting for some period after first rising from sleep find that they feel best this way. Many who grew up on dairy farms report that they would all rise well before sunrise (4 a.m.) and work for a good four hours before a hearty breakfast at 8 a.m. Others find that it is ideal to exercise vigorously (walk, run, swim, etc.) and then do some form of breathing and meditation practice before eating. We don't know what time Mr. Wattles was assuming you would awaken if you were to wait until noon to eat, but his point about waiting until you are actually hungry is well advised.

If you find that you feel ill on waking, or after a prolonged period without food, and you do not have a blood sugar problem, the most likely explanation is that your body is reacting to something you ate. Try experimenting with different foods.

Another less common possibility relates to toxicity. If you have been exposed to nasty chemicals (for example, you smoked for years or your parents did, or you grew up in an area where chemicals were sprayed to kill mosquitoes or agricultural pests), residues of these chemicals are stored in your fat cells. When your body burns the fat, the chemicals are released into your blood, and you feel the effects. If you think this is going on, visit a naturopathic doctor for guidance.

Second, the standard American breakfast of 1910 that Mr. Wattles is warning against was a large, heavy meal including some combination of ham, sausage, eggs, beef steaks, and pork chops along with biscuits and gravy or cornbread, pastries or bread and jam, and often fruit pie. It is not surprising that a person would feel better avoiding this gross overindulgence, especially if eaten before he was actually hungry!

Third, if you have some sort of blood sugar irregularity requiring more fre-quent meals, your body will let you know you are hungry. The vital aspect of this "when to eat" recommendation is to learn how to PAY ATTENTION TO YOUR BODY with the relaxed attitude of gratitude, trust, curiosity, and un-conditional love rather than being pushed around by habit, fear, anxiety, social customs, other people's schedules and other people's ideas about what is good for you.

Is Prolonged Fasting Safe?

If you are starved or emaciated, and have not eaten for days or weeks, is it safe to wait to eat until you feel hunger? There is a wide variety of physical, mental, and psychological conditions that may be involved in a person becoming starved or emaciated. Medical supervision by a doctor familiar with conditions like this is essential. In modern times, we are equipped with all sorts of testing and monitoring to more accu-rately guide a person through critical states. We also have methods of nourishment that bypass the digestive tract when a weakened person can't digest food. However, it is important to understand the source of Mr. Wattles' convic-tion that if you are not hungry, "food cannot be used, and that it is unnatural and wrong for you to eat." Wattles clearly drew many of his ideas about the effectiveness of medicine and eating habits from the works of Edward Hooker Dewey, M.D., who he names in the preface to this book. You can read fascinating excerpts from Dr. Dewey's 1900 book, The No-Breakfast Plan and The Fasting Cure, in the section "Historical Notes on When, What, and How to Eat" at the end of this book.

Should You Eat Only One Meal a Day?

Mr. Wattles says that in most cases a person will not have an "earned" hunger for more than one meal per day. This might be true if your one meal is high in fat and animal protein. However, we now know that perfect health requires nutrients which in most climates are found in fresh vegetables, fruits, nuts, seeds, and grains. Also, we know that fiber, found only in plant foods, is im-portant. Many of these foods, particularly the highest quality vegetables, are very low in calories. You would need to eat more than once per day to con-sume enough of these for perfect health.

As you learn to trust the "voice" of your body rather than your appetite (as described by Mr. Wattles), you will naturally want to eat what your body re-quires, when your body requires it. If you have never tried eating just once a day, try it. If you frequently find yourself getting so caught up in other activi-

ties that you "forget to eat," chances are you have trained your mind to ignore your body's needs for food, water, and even movement. Experimentation dur-ing a time of restful vacation may be the only way to discover how to listen to your body. If, on the other hand, you are in the habit of eating continuously, you also may have lost communication with your body. A fast of a full day or two may be required before you can detect true hunger.

Chapter 10.
What To Eat

The current sciences of medicine and hygiene have made no progress toward answering the question, What shall I eat? The contests between the vegetarians and the meat eaters, the cooked food advocates, raw food advocates, and various other "schools" of theorists, seem to be interminable. And from the mountains of evidence and argument piled up for and against each special theory, it is plain that if we depend on these scientists we shall never know what is the natural food of humans. Turning away from the whole controversy, then, we will ask the question of Nature herself, and we shall find that she has not left us without an answer.

On the question of what to eat, the answer is simple: God has made an abundance of perfect foods for every person in every place humans can live, and has given every person the physical and mental faculties to know what foods he should eat and how and when he should eat them. Whenever people have attempted to "improve" on Nature, they go wrong. For humanity does not yet know enough not to go wrong. Nature provides every person exactly what is needed for perfect health.

God has in reality practically settled the question as to what we shall eat. Many of these are the foods best for the requirements of the climate. These are the foods which will be the freshest when a person eats them, and therefore most filled with the life force. In acquiring these foods a person can be in closest association with the Principle of Life that created them. Therefore, a person need only ask himself what food grows and lives where he lives.

How shall a person know which of these foods to eat, according to his age, gender, ancestry, condition of health, exposure to cold, physical and mental activity? God provides a variety of foods in every zone, and provides a human being with hunger and taste.

A person needs food as a raw material for the Principle of Health in his own body to direct in providing energy, heat, defense, and tissue repair and growth. He needs protein, carbohydrates, fats, vitamins, and minerals. These are found in the flesh, milk, blood, eggs, bones, and organs of water and land creatures, and in the roots, and stems. God guides the masses of people to discover ways of procuring and preparing these foods in harmony with Nature. A person's own Principle of Health guides his hunger and taste to the particular foods that will fill its needs.

With all the various ways food is prepared, how shall a person know the proper way? He should procure and prepare his food in ways that cooperate with Nature. It is only when people work against Nature that they go wrong. To illustrate this point let us compare the health of people working in cooperation with Nature with the health of these same people working against Nature.

In every climate there are tribes who have learned over thousands of years the wisdom of nature and the best ways to gather, prepare, and eat the foods of the region in perfect harmony with the seasons and cycles of Nature. The perfect health of these people provides a shining example of what is possible in physical strength and endurance, perfect eyesight and teeth, longevity, skill and agility, mental development, morality, and overall well-being. Moreover, they have learned the secrets of healthy reproduction and child-rearing such that there are not only happy, healthy children, but the absence of unsociable behavior.

What secrets of eating are followed by these perfectly healthy people?

* They eat only foods that occur in nature or that can be simply made from these.
* They eat only the best foods, and parts of foods, with the greatest nutrient content.
* They eat both animal and plant foods.
* Many foods from both plant and animal sources are eaten raw.
* From wild animals, bones, and organs are as important as (and often preferred over) muscle meat.
* From domesticated animals, fresh milk (and in some cases, even blood) is drawn. When milk products are used, they are made from milk taken from vitally healthy animals after they have been well fed on newly growing spring grasses. Cheese, butter, and other milk products that can be stored for later use are made from this milk. During other seasons, the animals are fed the highest quality hay.
* For some groups, insects in both adult and immature forms are important food sources, even where other animal foods are available.

In zones near the sea, sea creatures are the source of animal food. Fish eggs are a rich source of nutrients. Where they are not available year-round, both the flesh and eggs of fish are dried for winter use in a way that preserves or increases nutrient content.

Plant foods are eaten liberally during the season in which they grow and are ripe. Where they are not growing year-round, some are preserved for winter use in ways that preserves their nutrients.

Sweet foods of all kinds are eaten only sparingly on special occasions. Refined sugar is avoided altogether, as are all foods made by adding refined sugar.

Land used for plant cultivation is fertilized liberally with natural substances, and allowed periods of rest.

Grains are eaten whole, or ground immediately before use. The entire grain is used.

Women are supplied with extra high nutrient diets for several months before marriage and pregnancy, and during pregnancy and lactation. Childbirth is carefully spaced three years apart so that the mother can nurse her child, then replenish her body in preparation for the next pregnancy.

• Young men are also fed extra-high nutrient diets in preparation for fathering children.

• Children are nursed, then given high nutrient foods to help them grow.

There are times of natural decrease in food supply, and ceremonial times, when the people eat less, or not at all.

The people actively participate in the physical pursuit of growing, gathering, hunting, and preparing their food. They have community ceremonies of gratitude and celebration.

These are the practices of the healthiest people on earth. What happens when these same people abandon their way of living and eating and replace their foods with unnatural foods? They develop disease, deformity, misery, and unsociable behavior.

What are the unnatural foods that cause these effects?

They are refined and preserved foods from which natural life has been removed or lost, or sugar and flavors added to hide the absence of nutrients. They are foods so old that no life force remains in them. They are foods from unhealthy plants and animals, containing life force that bears the impression of weakness or disease. What is needed for perfect health is vital food, brimming with life force, eaten according to the practices of healthy people.

How shall the modern city dweller acquire this vital food and incorporate these practices into his life? First is to remember that he is to eat the food Nature provides in the zone in which he lives. He must align himself with the Principle of Life with gratitude that there is abundant food for all and with faith that he will be perfectly guided to the best sources available in his area. Perfect health requires a relationship with the Source of all food with faith, gratitude, and joy. Food must be gathered with the attitude of more life to all and less to none.

A person must either learn to grow and gather, raise animals, hunt and fish, or find those who do. If he does not procure his own food directly from Nature, he must form a friendly relationship with those who do. He can then knowingly choose to deal with those who operate in harmony with Nature, exercising gratitude and wisdom.

The person who does not know how to identify a farmer or hunter following the natural laws of producing and finding food can be guided by these simple concepts: Choosing your food providers:

1   The food provider is healthy, happy, and of a generous spirit.

2   He uses no poisons of any kind in the production of foods.

3   If he raises animals, they are healthy and treated with kindness, respect, and gratitude. They are fed only the best foods for their health, not for abnor-mal growth or food production. They are not confined in unhealthy condi-tions, but given freedom to move about normally, and only sheltered for their protection.

4   If he fishes or hunts, he catches or kills lake, river, land or sea creatures in their natural environment. He uses means that ensure the healthy survival of all the species caught, whether or not they are the ones to be eaten.

5   If he farms, he uses only healthy, living soil uncontaminated by previous poisons. He replenishes the life of the soil so that his crops are rich in natural nutrients. His crops and soil are so healthy that they do not attract pests, and he farms in such a way birds and other creatures eating the insects on his farm are unharmed. Any water running off his land contains no chemicals that will harm any

other part of life. These are the characteristics of a person who knows the laws of Nature in the production and procurement of food.

You must also know how to determine the correct people with whom to associate in any other steps of obtaining your food. Do not associate with anyone in the process of procuring food who speaks of disease, fear, or lack in any way. Associate only with those who gratefully and joyfully appreciate the life-giving qualities of food, are happy to grow it, har-vest it, prepare it, serve it, eat it, and know that there is an abundance of the best food for all. This is important whether you are dealing with someone who is selling you land on which to farm, or a farmer, or butcher, or truck driver, or store clerk, or cook, or waiter in a restaurant.

You must not eat foods produced or transported carelessly, or treated in any other way than as precious, life-giving substances. This is easily accomplished when you are the one procuring the food from its natural source or if you are in direct and harmonious relationship with all those who are.

The city dweller who thinks it is too difficult or too expensive to obtain food in this way need only review The Science of Getting Rich. All his doubts will there be answered. He will be guided in the correct manner of acquiring all the money he wants, and in attracting to himself all other resources he desires.

Once a person is supplied with a variety of vital foods from which to choose, how shall he know what to eat at a given meal? Here is the only needed guide-line: Eat what your body wants. Your body wants what the Principle of Health requires to create perfect health.

What your body wants is determined very simply. The thought of the food, when you are truly hungry, is appealing. The taste of the food while chewing it is pleasant. After eating, your body feels energized and satisfied. There is no sleepiness, irritability, congestion, pain, discomfort of any kind, from the mo-ment you begin to eat until the next day. Over a period of days, weeks and months, you continue to feel well.

This is how you will know you are eating the correct foods. Then you will not need to give the least thought to what you should or should not eat. You will want the right foods. The Principle of Health in your own body will guide you to know what to eat just as surely as it will guide you to know when to eat.

If you do not eat until you have an EARNED hunger, you will not find your taste demanding unnatural or unhealthy foods. If you make an association with your source of food that brings joy and gratitude, you will further increase your desire to eat what is natural and healthy.

It is when a person becomes lazy and allows himself to be tempted by taste and convenience, that he pays the price of decreased health. When you learn to cooperate with Nature you will want what is good for you, and you will eat what you want. This you can do with perfect results if you eat in the right way, and how to do this will be explained in the next chapter.

Chapter 11.
How To Eat

It is a settled fact that a person naturally chews his food. The few faddists who maintain that we should bolt our nourishment, after the manner of the dog and others of the lower animals, can no longer get a hearing. We know that we should chew our food. And if it is natural that we should chew our food, the more thoroughly we chew it the more completely natural the process must be. If you will chew every mouthful to a liquid, you need not be in the least concerned as to whether you are getting enough nutrients, for you have already chosen the best foods according to Natural Law.

Whether or not this chewing shall be an irksome and laborious task or a most enjoyable process depends upon the mental attitude in which you come to the table. If your mind and attitude are on other things, or if you are anxious or wor-ried about business or domestic affairs, you will find it almost impossible to eat without bolting more or less of your food. You must learn to live so scientifically that you will have no business or domestic cares to worry about. This you can do.

You must also arrange your life so that you are not in the presence of others who distract from the enjoyment of your meal. This way, you can learn to give your undivided attention to the act of eating while at the table. The matter of eating only when in a peaceful state of mind must be emphasized. You must focus on gratitude before eating the food on your table and on the full enjoyment of each bite while eating. After eating, you must again focus on gratitude for the vital force from the food supplied to you through the One Living Substance. These mental actions will assist in the physical extraction of vital force from your food, and in bringing the Principle of Health within you into full Constructive Activity.

You must therefore eat with an eye single to the purpose of getting all the enjoyment you can from that meal. Dismiss everything else from your mind, and do not let anything take your attention from the food and its taste until your meal is finished. Be cheerfully confident, for if you follow these instructions you may KNOW that the food you eat is exactly the right food, and that it will "agree" with you to perfection: Sit down to the table with confident cheerfulness, and take a moderate portion of the food. Take whatever thing looks most desirable to you. Do not select some food because you think it will be good for you — select that which will taste good to you. If you are to get well and stay well, you must drop the idea of doing things because they are good for your health, and do things because you want to do them. Select the food you want most, gratefully give thanks to God that you have learned how to eat it in such a way that digestion shall be perfect, and take a moderate mouthful of it.

Do not fix your attention on the act of chewing; fix it on the TASTE of the food. And taste and enjoy it until it is reduced to a liquid state and passes down your throat by involuntary swallowing. No matter how long it takes, do not think of the time. Think of the taste. Do not allow your eyes to wander over the table, speculating as to what you shall eat next. Do not worry for fear there is not enough, and that you will not get your share of everything. Do not anticipate the taste of the next thing. Keep your mind centered on the taste of what you have in your mouth. And that is all of it.

Scientific and healthful eating is a delightful process after you have learned how to do it, and after you have overcome the bad old habit of gobbling down your food unchewed. It is best not to have too much conversation going on while eating. Be cheerful, but not talkative. Do the talking afterward. In most cases, some use of the will is required to form the habit of correct eating. The bolting habit is an unnatural one, and is without doubt mostly the result of fear. Fear that we will be robbed of our food, fear that we will not get our share of the good things, fear that we will lose precious time — these are the causes of haste. Then there is anticipation of the dainties that are to come for dessert and the consequent desire to get at them as quickly as possible. And there is mental abstraction, or thinking of other matters while eating. All these must be overcome.

When you find that your mind is wandering, call a halt. Think for a moment of the food and of how good it tastes, of the perfect digestion and assimilation that are going to follow the meal, and begin again. Begin again and again, though you must do so 20 times in the course of a single meal. And again and again, though you must do so every meal for weeks and months. It is perfectly certain that you CAN form the "Fletcher habit"* if you persevere, and when you have formed it, you will experience a healthful pleasure you have never known. This is a vital point, and I must not leave it until I have thoroughly impressed it upon your mind. Given the right materials, perfectly prepared, the Principle of Health will positively build you a perfectly healthy body, and you cannot prepare the materials perfectly in any other way than the one I am describing.

If you are to have perfect health, you MUST eat in just this way. You can, and the doing of it is only a matter of a little perseverance. What use for you to talk of mental control unless you will govern yourself in so simple a matter as ceasing to bolt your food? What use to talk of concentration unless you can keep your mind on the act of eating for so short a space as 15 or 20 minutes, especially with all the pleasures of taste to help you?

*See Glossary at end of book.

Go on, and conquer. In a few weeks, or months, as the case may be, you will find the habit of scientific eating becoming fixed, and soon you will be in so splendid a condition, mentally and physically, that nothing would induce you to return to the bad old way.

We have seen that if a person will think only thoughts of perfect health, his internal functions will be performed in a healthy manner, and we have seen that in order to think thoughts of health, a person must perform the voluntary functions in a healthy manner. The most important of the voluntary functions is that of eating, and we see, so far, no special difficulty in eating in a perfectly healthy way.

I will summarize the instructions as to when to eat, what to eat, and how to eat, with the reasons why:

NEVER eat until you have an EARNED hunger, no matter how long you go without food. This is based on the fact that whenever food is needed in the system, if there is power to digest it, the sub-conscious mind announces the need by the sensation of hunger. Learn to distinguish between genuine hunger and the gnawing and craving sensations caused by unnatural appetite. Hunger is never a disagreeable feel-ing, accompanied by weakness, faintness, or gnawing feelings at the stomach. It is a pleasant, anticipatory desire for food. It does not come at certain hours or at stated intervals. It only comes when the body is ready to receive, digest, and assimilate food.

Eat whatever foods you want, making your selection from the full variety of the best foods found in the zone in which you live. The Supreme Intelligence has guided humanity to the selection of these foods, and they are the right ones. I am referring, of course, to the foods which are taken to satisfy hunger, not to those which have been contrived merely to gratify appetite or perverted taste. The instinct which has guided people to make use of the great staples of food to satisfy their hunger is a divine one. God has made no mistake; if you eat these foods you will not go wrong. Eat your food with cheerful confidence in a pleasant atmosphere, and get all the pleasure that is to be had from the taste of every mouthful. Chew each morsel to a liquid, keeping your attention fixed on the enjoyment of the pro-cess. This is the only way to eat in a perfectly complete and successful manner; and when anything is done in a completely successful manner, the general result cannot be a failure.

In the attainment of health, the law is the same as in the attainment of riches: if you make each act a success in itself, the sum of all your acts must be a success. When you eat in the mental attitude I have described, and in the manner I have described, nothing can be added to the process — it is done in a perfect manner, and it is successfully done. And if eating is successfully done, digestion, assimilation, and the building of a healthy body are successfully begun. We next take up the question of the quantity of food required.

Editor's Notes
    Is It Appetite or Hunger?
Mr. Wattles states: "Hunger is never a disagreeable feeling, accompanied by weakness, faintness, or gnawing feelings at the stomach. It is a pleasant, anticipatory desire for food."

First, understand that Mr. Wattles is referring to the hunger sensation in people who are able to eat when hungry. This does not apply to those who are hungry but have been deprived of food, such as in famine.

Second, this statement may be confusing for those with food allergies or food sensitivities, eating disorders, blood sugar regulation problems, or other biochemical imbalances. Consuming sweets, artificial foods, or alcohol also con-fuses hunger sensation. I will address those briefly here, and recommend that you work with a naturopathic doctor, dietitian, or nutritionist if you have any of these issues.

If you have food allergies or sensitivities (other food reactions) you may experience symptoms of weakness, faintness, gnawing feelings, irritability, and a host of other "disagreeable" feelings only a couple of hours after eating. Often you will crave the very foods to which you are sensitive or allergic. Many people who are sensitive to wheat and/or sugar crave bread or sweets. This would be "unnatural appetite."

Alcohol and sweets (including juice, sodas, and other sweet drinks) will usually create an "unnatural appetite." After consuming them, you usually want to eat more than you would eat otherwise.

Some people are familiar with the problem of overgrowth of intestinal yeast. The yeast creates an alcohol (a metabolic byproduct of the yeast) which is ab-sorbed into the bloodstream, and causes effects similar to drinking alcohol — "unnatural appetite." This and other biochemical imbalances are best diag-nosed by a doctor.

Filling up on foods with low nutrient content or "empty calories" (common in artificial or highly processed foods) will leave the body needing nutrients. The hunger signal is confused because the body wants the nutrients but does not need the calories. Usually a person continues to eat to try to fill the lack, but gets caught up in craving more empty foods. This would be "unnatural appetite." The obvious solution is to eat naturally high-nutrient foods.

If you have a problem with blood sugar regulation (hypoglycemia, diabetes) your body will signal its need for food with these same symptoms of weakness, faintness, gnawing feelings, and irritability. In this case there is actual hunger. You should work with a doctor who specializes in using nutrition to help regulate blood sugar.

If you have an eating disorder such as bingeing, bulemia, or anorexia, it may be impossible for you to detect true hunger. Likewise, if you have a physical condition or are taking medicine that causes nausea or otherwise affects your desire for food, hunger may not be reliable. In these cases, a doctor should guide you in applying Mr. Wattles' eating plan.

Chapter 12.
Hunger and Appetites

It is very easy to find the correct answer to the question, How much shall I eat? You are never to eat until you have an earned hunger, and you are to stop eating the instant you BEGIN to feel that your hunger is abating. Never gorge yourself. Never eat to repletion. When you begin to feel that your hunger is satisfied, know that you have enough. For until you have enough, you will continue to feel the sensation of hunger.

If you eat as directed in the last chapter, it is probable that you will begin to feel satisfied before you have taken half your usual amount, but stop there, all the same. No matter how delightfully attractive the dessert, or how tempting the pie or pudding, do not eat a mouthful of it if you find that your hunger has been in the least degree assuaged by the other foods you have taken.

Whatever you eat after your hunger begins to abate is taken to gratify taste and appetite, not hunger and is not called for by nature at all. It is therefore excess — mere debauchery — and it cannot fail to work mischief. This is a point you will need to watch with nice discrimination, for the habit of eating purely for sensual gratification is very deeply rooted with most of us. The usual "dessert" of sweet and tempting foods is prepared solely with a view to inducing people to eat after hunger has been satisfied, and all the effects are evil. For the effect of eating these unwholesome foods is often an increase in appetite.

The same is true of alcohol taken before eating. Both will trick you to eat far more than you would otherwise want, and make it difficult to focus your attention on the satisfaction of your true hunger. You will find that if you eat as directed in the preceding chapters, the plainest food will soon come to taste like kingly fare to you, for your sense of taste, like all your other senses, will become so acute with the general improvement in your condition that you will find new delights in common things.

No glutton ever enjoyed a meal like the person who eats for hunger only, who gets the most out of every mouthful, and who stops on the instant that he feels the edge taken from his hunger. The first intimation that hunger is abating is the signal from the subconscious mind that it is time to quit.

The average person who takes up this plan of living will be greatly surprised to learn how little food is really required to keep the body in perfect condition.

The amount depends upon the work — upon how much muscular exercise is taken, and upon the extent to which the person is exposed to cold.

The woodchopper who goes into the forest in the winter time and swings his axe all day can eat two full meals, but the brain worker who sits all day on a chair, in a warm room, does not need one-third and often not one-tenth as much. Most woodchoppers eat two or three times as much, and most brain workers from three to ten times as much as nature calls for, and the elimination of this vast amount of surplus rubbish from their systems is a tax on vital power which in time depletes their energy and leaves them an easy prey to so-called disease.

Get all possible enjoyment out of the taste of your food, but never eat anything merely because it tastes good. And on the instant that you feel that your hunger is less keen, stop eating.

If you will consider for a moment, you will see that there is positively no other way for you to settle these various food questions than by adopting the plan here laid down for you. As to the proper time to eat, there is no other way to decide than to say that you should eat whenever you have an EARNED HUNGER. It is a self-evident proposition that that is the right time to eat, and that any other is a wrong time to eat.

As to what to eat, God has given the Biblical dietary laws that the people will eat, the best products of the zones in which they live. The staple foods of your particular zone are the right foods for you, and God, has taught them how best to prepare these foods by cooking and otherwise.

And as to how to eat, you know that you must chew your food in a peaceful state of mind, and if food must be chewed, then reason tells us that the more thorough and perfect the operation the better.

I repeat that success in anything is attained by making each separate act a success in itself. If you make each action, however small and unimportant, a thoroughly successful action, your day's work as a whole cannot result in fail-ure. If you make the actions of each day successful, the sum total of your life cannot be failure.

A great success is the result of doing a large number of little things, and do-ing each one in a perfectly successful way. If every thought is a healthy thought, and if every action of your life is performed in a healthy way, you must soon attain to perfect health. It is impossible to devise a way in which you can perform the act of eating more successfully, and in a manner more in accord with the laws of life, than by chewing every mouthful to a liquid, enjoying the taste fully, and keeping a cheerful confidence the while. Nothing can be added to make the process more successful, while if anything be subtracted, the process will not be a completely healthy one.

In the matter of how much to eat, you will also see that there could be no other guide so natural, so safe, and so reliable as the one I have prescribed — to stop eating on the instant you feel that your hunger begins to abate. The subconscious mind may be trusted with implicit reliance to inform us when food is needed, and it may be trusted as implicitly to inform us when the need has been supplied. If ALL food is eaten for hunger, and NO food is taken merely to gratify taste, you will never eat too much, and if you eat whenever you have an EARNED hunger, you will always eat enough.

By carefully reading the summing up in the following chapter, you will see that the requirements for eating in a perfectly healthy way are really very few and simple.

The matter of drinking in a natural way may be dismissed here with a very few words. If you wish to be exactly and rigidly scientific, drink nothing but water, drink only when you are thirsty, drink whenever you are thirsty, and stop as soon as you feel that your thirst begins to abate. But if you are living rightly in regard to eating, it will not be necessary to practice asceticism or great self-denial in the matter of drinking. You can take an occasional cup of weak coffee without harm. You can, to a reasonable extent, follow the customs of those around you. Do not get the soda fountain habit. Do not drink merely to tickle your palate with sweet liquids. Be sure that you take a drink of water whenever you feel thirst. Never be too lazy, too indifferent, or too busy to get a drink of water when you feel the least thirst. If you obey this rule, you will have little inclination to take strange and unnatural drinks. Drink only to satisfy thirst, drink whenever you feel thirst, and stop drinking as soon as you feel thirst abating. That is the perfectly healthy way to supply the body with the necessary fluid material for its internal processes.

Editor's Note
   Coffee?
   If your standard breakfast is a cup of coffee and you don't feel awake until you have it, or you use coffee to perk yourself up during the day, or if you feel angry and threatened at the thought of not being able to have it, you are using coffee like a drug. This is definitely NOT the occasional cup of weak coffee that Mr. Wattles says is OK if you are otherwise following the eating plan.
If you want health, focus on building your desire for health so that it is greater than your desire for anything that does not support health.

Chapter 13.
In a Nutshell

Here is a Cosmic Life which permeates, penetrates, and fills the interspaces of the universe, being in and through all things. This Life is not merely a vibration, or form of energy — it is a Living Substance. All things are made from it. It is All, and in all. This Substance thinks, and it assumes the form of that which it thinks about. The thought of a form, in this substance, creates the form; the thought of a motion institutes the motion. The visible universe, with all its forms and motions, exists because it is in the thought of Original Substance.

A human being is a form of Original Substance and can think original thoughts, and within himself a person's thoughts have controlling or forma-tive power. The thought of a condition produces that condition; the thought of a motion institutes that motion. So long as a person thinks of the conditions and motions of disease, so long will the conditions and motions of disease exist within him. If a person will think only of perfect health, the Principle of Health within him will maintain normal conditions.

To be well, a person must form a conception of perfect health, and hold thoughts harmonious with that conception as regards himself and all things. He must think only of healthy conditions and functioning. He must not permit a thought of unhealthy or abnormal conditions or functioning to find lodgment in his mind at any time.

In order to think only of healthy conditions and functioning, a person must perform the voluntary acts of life in a perfectly healthy way. He cannot think perfect health so long as he knows that he is living in a wrong or unhealthy way, or even so long as he has doubts as to whether or not he is living in a healthy way.

A person cannot think thoughts of perfect health while his voluntary functions are performed in the manner of one who is sick. The voluntary functions of life are eating, drinking, breathing, and sleeping. When a person thinks only of healthy conditions and functioning, and performs these externals in a perfectly healthy manner, he must have perfect health.

In eating, a person must learn to be guided by his hunger. He must distinguish between hunger and appetite, and between hunger and the cravings of habit. He must NEVER eat unless he feels an EARNED HUNGER.
He must learn that genuine hunger is never present after natural sleep, and that the demand for an early morning meal is purely a matter of habit and ap-petite; and he must not begin his day by eating in violation of natural law. He must wait until he has an Earned Hunger, which, in most cases, will make his first meal come at about the noon hour.

No matter what his condition, vocation, or circumstances, he must make it his rule not to eat until he has an EARNED HUNGER, and he may remember that it is far better to fast for several hours after he has become hungry than to eat before he begins to feel hunger. It will not hurt you to go hungry for a few hours, even though you are working hard, but it will hurt you to fill your stom-ach when you are not hungry, whether you are working or not. If you never eat until you have an Earned

Hunger, you may be certain that in so far as the time of eating is concerned, you are proceeding in a perfectly healthy way. This is a self-evident proposition.

As to what he shall eat, a person must have faith in God, and trust God's ability to guide your taste to that which your body requires. Do not worry over the controversies as to the relative merits of cooked and raw foods, of vegetables and meats, or as to your need for carbohydrates and proteins.

Eat only when you have an earned hunger, and then take the best foods of the healthy people in the zone in which you live, and have perfect confidence that the results will be good. They will be.

Do not seek for luxuries, or for things imported or fixed up to tempt the taste. Stick to the plain foods, and when these do not "taste good," fast until they do. Then you will be functioning in a perfectly healthy manner, so far as what to eat is concerned. I repeat, if you have no hunger or taste for the plain foods, do not eat at all. Wait until hunger comes. Go without eating until the plainest food tastes good to you, and then begin your meal with what you like best.

In deciding how to eat, a person must be guided by reason. We can see that the abnormal states of hurry and worry produced by wrong thinking about business and similar things have led us to form the habit of eating too fast, and chewing too little.

We know that an angry or distracting atmosphere upsets the process of digestion. Reason tells us that food should be chewed, and that the more thoroughly it is chewed the better it is prepared for the chemistry of digestion. Furthermore, we can see that the person who eats slowly and chews his food to a liquid, keeping his mind on the process and giving it his undivided attention, will enjoy more of the pleasure of taste than he who bolts his food with his mind on something else.

To eat in a perfectly healthy manner, a person must concentrate his attention on the act with cheerful enjoyment and confidence. He must taste his food, and he must reduce each mouthful to a liquid before swallowing it. The foregoing instructions, if followed, make the function of eating completely perfect. Nothing can be added as to what, when, and how.

In the matter of how much to eat, a person must be guided by the same inward intelligence, or Principle of Health, which tells him when food is wanted. He must stop eating in the moment that he feels hunger abating; he must not eat beyond this point to gratify taste. If he ceases to eat in the instant that the inward demand for food ceases he will never overeat, and the function of supplying the body with food will be performed in a perfectly healthy manner.

The matter of eating naturally is a very simple one; there is nothing in all the foregoing that cannot be easily practiced by anyone. This method, put into practice, will infallibly result in perfect digestion and assimilation, and all anxi-ety and careful thought concerning the matter can at once be dropped from the mind. Whenever you have an earned hunger, eat with thankfulness from the variety of natural foods before you, chewing each mouthful to a liquid, and stopping when you feel the edge taken from your hunger.

The importance of the mental attitude is sufficient to justify an additional word.

While you are eating, as at all other times, think only of healthy conditions and normal functioning. Enjoy what you eat. If you carry on a conversation at the table, talk of the goodness of the food, and of the pleasure it is giving you. Never mention that you dislike this or that. Speak only of those things which you like. Never discuss the wholesomeness or unwholesomeness of foods. Never mention or think of unwholesomeness at all.

If there is anything on the table for which you do not care, pass it by in silence, or with a word of commendation. Never criticize or object to anything. Eat your food with gladness and with singleness of heart, praising God and giving thanks. Let your watchword be perseverance. Whenever you fall into the old way of hasty eating, or of wrong thought and speech, bring yourself up short and begin again.

It is of the most vital importance to you that you should be a self-controlling and self-directing person, and you can never hope to become so unless you can master yourself in so simple and fundamental a matter as the manner and method of your eating. If you cannot control yourself in this, you cannot control yourself in anything that will be worthwhile. On the other hand, if you carry out the foregoing instructions, you may rest in the assurance that in so far as right thinking and right eating are concerned you are living in a perfectly scientific way, and you may also be assured that if you practice what is prescribed in the following chapters you will quickly build your body into a condition of perfect health.

Chapter 14.
Breathing

The function of breathing is a vital one, and it immediately concerns the continuance of life. We can live many hours without sleeping, and many days without eating or drinking, but only a few minutes without breathing.

The act of breathing is involuntary, but the manner of it and the provision of the proper conditions for its healthy performance fall within the scope of voli-tion. A person will continue to breathe involuntarily, but he can voluntarily determine what he shall breathe, and how deeply and thoroughly he shall breathe. And he can, of his own volition, keep the physical mechanism in con-dition for the perfect performance of the function.

It is essential, if you wish to breathe in a perfectly healthy way, that the physical machinery used in the act should be kept in good condition. You must keep your spine moderately straight, and the muscles of your chest must be flexible and free in action. You cannot breathe in the right way if your shoulders are greatly stooped forward and your chest hollow and rigid. Sitting or standing at work in a slightly stooping position tends to produce a hollow chest. So does lifting heavy weights — or light weights.

The tendency of work, of almost all kinds, is to pull the shoulders forward, curve the spine, and flatten the chest, and if the chest is greatly flattened, full and deep breathing becomes impossible and perfect health is out of the question.

Various gymnastic exercises have been devised to counteract the effect of stooping while at work, such as hanging by the hands from a swing or trapeze bar, or sitting on a chair with the feet under some heavy article of furniture and bending backward until the head touches the floor, and so on. All these are good enough in their way, but very few people will follow them long enough and regularly enough to accomplish any real gain in physique. The taking of "health exercises" of any kind is burdensome and unnecessary.

There is a more natural, simpler, and much better way.

This better way is to keep yourself straight, and to breathe deeply. Let your mental conception of yourself be that you are a perfectly straight person, and whenever the matter comes to your mind, be sure that you instantly expand your chest, throw back your shoulders, and "straighten up." Whenever you do this, slowly draw in your breath until you fill your lungs to their utmost capacity. "Crowd in" all the air you possibly can, and while holding it for an instant in the lungs, throw your shoulders still further back, and stretch your chest. At the same time try to pull your spine forward between the shoulders. Then let the air go easily.

This is the one great exercise for keeping the chest full, flexible, and in good condition. Straighten up, fill your lungs FULL, stretch your chest and straighten your spine, and exhale easily. And this exercise you must repeat, in season and out of season, at all times and in all places, until you form a habit of doing it. You can easily do so.

Whenever you step out of doors into the fresh, pure air, BREATHE. When you are at work, and think of yourself and your position, BREATHE. When you are in company, and are reminded of the matter, BREATHE. When you are awake in the night, BREATHE. No matter where you are or what you are doing, whenever the idea comes to your mind, straighten up and BREATHE. If you walk to and from your work, take this exercise all the way. It will soon become a delight to you, and you will keep it up, not for the sake of health, but as a matter of pleasure.

Do not consider this a "health exercise." Never take health exercises or do gymnastics to make you well. To do so is to recognize sickness as a present fact or as a possibility, which is precisely what you must not do. The people who are always taking exercises for their health are always thinking about being sick. It ought to be a matter of pride with you to keep your spine straight and strong — as much so as it is to keep your face clean.

Keep your spine straight, and your chest full and flexible for the same rea-son that you keep your hands clean and your nails manicured — because it is slovenly to do otherwise. Do it without a thought of sickness, present or pos-sible. You must either be crooked and unsightly or you must be straight, and if you are straight your breathing will take care of itself. You will find the matter of health exercises referred to again in a future chapter. It is essential, however, that you should breathe AIR. It appears to be the intention of nature that the lungs should receive air containing its regular percentage of oxygen and not greatly contaminated by other gases, or by filth of any kind.

Do not allow yourself to think that you are compelled to live or work where the air is not fit to breathe. If your house cannot be properly ventilated, move. And if you are employed where the air is bad, get another job — you can, by practicing the methods given in the preceding volume of this series,
The Science of Getting Rich. If no one would consent to work in bad air, employers would speedily see to it that all work rooms were properly

ventilated. The worst air is that filled with poisonous chemical gases.*

*This includes tobacco smoke and most other smoke; fumes from paint, plastic, gasoline and other petroleum products, solvents, glues, carpets and furniture made from artificial substances, and even household cleaners.

Next to that is air heavily charged with mold, asbestos, or factory dust particles. After that is air from which the oxygen has been exhausted by breathing — as that of airplanes, churches and theaters where crowds of people congregate, and the outlet and supply of air are poor.

Then there is air containing other natural gases than oxygen and hydrogen — sewer gas and the effiuvium from decaying things. Air that contains household dust or pollen may be endured better than any of these. Small particles of organic matter other than food are more easily thrown off from the lungs than gases, which go into the blood. I speak advisedly when I say "other than food." Air is largely a food. It is the most thoroughly alive thing we take into the body. Every breath carries life. The odors from earth, grass, tree, flower, plant, and from cooking foods are foods in themselves. They are minute particles of the substances from which they come, and are often so attenuated that they pass directly from the lungs into the blood, and are assimilated without digestion. And the atmosphere is permeated with the One Original Substance, which is life itself.

Consciously recognize this whenever you think of your breathing, and think that you are breathing in life. You really are, and conscious recognition helps the process. See to it that you do not breathe air containing poisonous gases, and that you do not rebreathe the air which has been used by yourself or others.

That is all there is to the matter of breathing correctly. Keep your spine straight and your chest flexible, and breathe pure air, recognizing with thankfulness the fact that you breathe in the Eternal Life. That is not difficult, and beyond these things give little thought to your breathing except to thank G-d that you have learned how to do it perfectly.

Editor's Note

On breathing pure air:

Most of us today are familiar with the health risks of exposure to cigarette and other tobacco smoke, both to the smokers and to those around them. Most have heard stories of those with lung disease who have trouble in polluted air. And most of us will take action to avoid foul-smelling air or air that causes us immediate ill effects. However, in my experience, most people are entirely ignorant of, or extremely careless about, their own protection from polluted air that appears to cause no immediate ill effect but can lead to great disability.

When is the last time you saw someone wear a respirator mask when painting the bathroom or applying pesticides in the garden? We live in an environment filled with tens of thousands of highly toxic chemicals that have never been tested for their health effects. Modern buildings with recirculated air may also contain toxic mold resulting from hidden water damage.

What should you do with this information? This, and more, is all true, but to focus our attention on it is exactly what Mr. Wattles warns us NOT to do. How can you take intelligent action without becoming fearfully vigilant?

The simplest approach is to focus your attention on breathing clean, fresh air. Arrange your life so you have maximum fresh air at all times. Choose ways of doing everything that avoid polluting or recirculating the air you breathe at home, at work, in your car, and outdoors. If you MUST come into contact with chemicals or airborne particles, wear a proper mask so you don't breathe in any of the poisonous stuff.

In situations in which you cannot be physically protected from an exposure, you must use mental action. Do not spend a moment thinking about how toxic those bus fumes are or how your health is being harmed by that person smok-ing a cigarette. Think instead, Ah! Fresh air is just around the corner — and then, as soon as you can, go to where the air is clean.

If you are in a situation in which the air seems less than pure, and you cannot immediately leave, focus your attention on all the pure molecules of air amongst the others. If the air is able to sustain life, that means there is plenty of good air for you to breathe, and you must think only of the good air entering your lungs.

Chapter 15.
Sleep

ital power is renewed in sleep. Every living thing sleeps. Humans, ani
mals, reptiles, fish, and insects sleep, and even plants have regular peri
ods of slumber. And this is because it is in sleep that we come into such contact with the Principle of Life in nature that our own lives may be renewed. It is in sleep that our brains are recharged with vital energy and the Principle of Health within us is given new strength. It is of the first importance, then, that we should sleep in a natural, normal, and perfectly healthy manner.

Studying sleep, we note that the breathing is much deeper and more forcible and rhythmic than in the waking state. Much more air is inspired when asleep than when awake, and this tells us that the Principle of Health requires large quantities of some element in the atmosphere for the process of renewal.

If you would surround sleep with natural conditions, then, the first step is to see that you have an unlimited supply of fresh and pure air to breathe. Physi-cians have found that sleeping in the pure air of out-of-doors is very effective in the treatment of pulmonary troubles, and, taken in connection with the Way of Living and Thinking prescribed in this book, you will find that it is just as effective in curing every other sort of trouble.

Do not take any half-way measures in this matter of securing pure air while you sleep. Ventilate your bedroom thoroughly — so thoroughly that it will be practically the same as sleeping out of doors. Have a door or window open wide; have one open on each side of the room, if possible. If you cannot have a good draught of air across the room, pull the head of your bed close to the open window, so that the air from without may come fully into your face. No matter how cold or unpleasant the weather, have a window open, and open wide, and try to get a circulation of pure air through the room. Pile on the bedclothes, if necessary, to keep you warm, but have an unlimited supply of fresh air from out of doors. This is the first great requisite for healthy sleep.

The brain and nerve centers cannot be thoroughly vitalized if you sleep in "dead" or stagnant air. You must have the living atmosphere, vital with nature's Principle of Life. I repeat, do not make any compromise in this matter. Ventilate your sleeping room completely, and see that there is a circulation of out-door air through it while you sleep. You are not sleeping in a perfectly healthy way if you shut the doors and windows of your sleeping room, whether in winter or summer. Have fresh air. If you are where there is no fresh air, move. If your bedroom cannot be ventilated, get into another house.

Next in importance is the mental attitude in which you go to sleep. It is well to sleep intelligently, purposefully, knowing what you do it for. Lie down thinking that sleep is an infallible vitalizer, and go to sleep with a confident faith that your strength is to be renewed, that you will awake full of vitality and health. Put purpose into your sleep as you do into your eating. Give the matter your attention for a few minutes, as you go to rest.

Do not seek your couch with a discouraged or depressed feeling; go there joyously, to be made whole. Do not forget the exercise of gratitude in going to sleep. Before you close your eyes, give thanks to G-d for having shown you the way to perfect health, and go to sleep with this grateful thought uppermost in your mind.

The bedtime prayer of thanksgiving is a mighty good thing. It puts the Principle of Health within you into communication with its source, from which it is to receive new power while you are in the silence of unconsciousness. You may see that the requirements for perfectly healthy sleep are not difficult. First, to see that you breathe pure air from out of doors while you sleep, and, second, to put the Within into touch with the Living Substance by a few minutes of grateful meditation as you go to bed. Observe these requirements, go to sleep in a thankful and confident frame of mind, and all will be well.

If you have insomnia, do not let it worry you. While you lie awake, form your conception of health. Meditate with thankfulness on the abundant life which is yours. Breathe, and feel perfectly confident that you will sleep in due time — and you will. Insomnia, like every other ailment, must give way before the Principle of Health aroused to full constructive activity by the course of thought and action herein described.

The reader will now comprehend that it is not at all burdensome or dis-agreeable to perform the voluntary functions of life in a perfectly healthy way. The perfectly healthy way is the easiest, simplest, most natural, and most pleasant way. The cultivation of health is not a work of art, difficulty, or strenuous labor. You have only to lay aside artificial observances of every kind and eat, drink, breathe, and sleep in the most natural and delightful way, and if you do this, thinking health and only health, you will certainly be well.

Chapter 16.
Supplementary Instructions

In forming a conception of health, it is necessary to think of the manner in which you would live and work if you were perfectly well and very strong — to imagine yourself doing things in the way of a perfectly well and very strong person, until you have a fairly good conception of what you would be if you were well.

Then take a mental and physical attitude in harmony with this conception, and do not depart from this attitude. You must unify yourself in thought with the thing you desire, and whatever state or condition you unify with yourself in thought will soon become unified with you in body. The scientific way is to sever relations with everything you do not want, and to enter into relations with everything you do want. Form a conception of perfect health, and relate yourself to this conception in word, act, and attitude.

Guard your speech. Make every word harmonize with the conception of perfect health. Never complain. Never say things like these: "I did not sleep well last night," "I have a pain in my side," "I do not feel at all well today," and so on. Say: "I am looking forward to a good night's sleep tonight," "I can see that I progress rapidly," and things of similar meaning. As far as everything which is connected with disease is concerned, your way is to forget it; and as far as everything which is connected with health is concerned, your way is to unify yourself with it in thought and speech.

This is the whole thing in a nutshell: make yourself one with Health in thought, word, and action, and do not connect yourself with sickness either by thought, word, or action. Do not read "doctor books" or medical literature, or the literature of those whose theories conflict with those herein set forth. To do so will certainly un-dermine your faith in the Way of Living upon which you have entered and cause you to again come into mental relations with disease. This book really gives you all that is required — nothing essential has been omitted, and practi-cally all the superfluous has been eliminated.

The Science of Being Well is an exact science, like arithmetic. Nothing can be added to the fundamental principles, and if anything be taken from them, a failure will result. If you follow strictly the way of living prescribed in this book, you will be well. And you certainly CAN follow this way, both in thought and action.

Relate not only yourself, but so far as possible all others, in your thoughts, to perfect health. Do not sympathize with people when they complain, or even when they are sick and suffering. Turn their thoughts into a constructive chan-nel if you can. Do all you can for their relief, but do it with the health thought in your mind.

Do not let people tell their woes and catalogue their symptoms to you. Turn the conversation to some other subject, or excuse yourself and go. Better be considered an unfeeling person than to have the disease thought forced upon you. When you are in company of people whose conversational stock-in-trade is sickness and kindred matters, ignore what they say and fall to offering a men-tal prayer of gratitude for your perfect health. And if that does not enable you to shut out their

141

thoughts, say good-by and leave them. No matter what they think or say, politeness does not require you to permit yourself to be poisoned by diseased or perverted thought. When we have a few more hundreds of thousands of enlightened thinkers who will not stay where people complain and talk sickness, the world will advance rapidly to-ward health. When you let people talk to you of sickness, you assist them to increase and multiply sickness.

What shall I do when I am in pain? Can one be in actual physical suffering and still think only thoughts of health? Yes. Do not resist pain; recognize that it is a good thing. Pain is caused by an effort of the Principle of Health to overcome some unnatural condition. This you must know and feel.

When you have a pain, think that a process of healing is going on in the affected part, and mentally assist and cooperate with it. Put yourself in full mental harmony with the power which is causing the pain — assist it, help it along. Do not hesitate, when necessary, to use hot fomentations and similar means to further the good work which is going on. If the pain is severe, lie down and give your mind to the work of quietly and easily cooperating with the force which is at work for your good.

This is the time to exercise gratitude and faith. Be thankful for the power of health which is causing the pain, and be certain that the pain will cease as soon as the good work is done. Fix your thoughts, with confidence, on the Principle of Health which is making such conditions within you that pain will soon be unnecessary. You will be surprised to find how easily you can conquer pain, and after you have lived for a time in this Scientific Way, pains and aches will be things unknown to you.

What shall I do when I am too weak for my work? Shall I drive myself beyond my strength, trusting in God to support me? Shall I go on, like the runner, expecting a "second wind?" No; better not. When you begin to live in this Way, you will probably not be of normal strength, and you will gradually pass from a low physical condition to a higher one. If you relate yourself mentally with health and strength, and perform the voluntary functions of life in a perfectly healthy manner, your strength will increase from day to day, but for a time you may have days when your strength is insufficient for the work you would like to do.

At such times rest and exercise gratitude. Recognize the fact that your strength is growing rapidly, and feel a deep thankfulness to God from whom it comes. Spend an hour of weakness in thanksgiving and rest, with full faith that great strength is at hand, and then get up and go on again. While you rest do not think of your present weakness; think of the strength that is coming.

Never, at any time, allow yourself to think that you are giving way to weakness. When you rest, as when you go to sleep, fix your mind on the Principle of Health which is building you into complete strength.

What shall I do about that great bugaboo which scares millions of people to death every year — constipation?

Do not worry. Read Horace Fletcher on The A.B.- Z. of Our Own Nutrition, and get the full force of his explanation of the fact that when you live on this scientific plan there will be much less matter to eliminate.* The material from the plant foods you are naturally guided to eat will take care of the matter.

*Relevant information from Fletcher's book is included in Historical Notes on When, What, and How to Eat at the end of this book.

The gross feeders who eat from three to ten times as much fat, meat, and starch as can be utilized in their systems have a great amount of waste to eliminate and not the plant materials to assist, but if you live in the manner we have de-scribed it will be otherwise with you.

If you eat only when you have an EARNED HUNGER, and chew every mouthful to a liquid, and if you stop eating the instant you BEGIN to be con-scious of an abatement of your hunger, you will so perfectly prepare your food for digestion and assimilation that practically all of it will be taken up by the absorbents, and there will be little remaining in the bowels to be excreted. If you are able to entirely banish from your memory all that you have read in "doctor books" and patent medicine advertisements concerning constipation, you need give the matter no further thought at all. The Principle of Health will take care of it.

But if your mind has been filled with fear-thought in regard to constipation, it may be well in the beginning for you to occasionally flush the colon with warm water. There is not the least need of doing it, except to make the process of your mental emancipation from fear a little easier; it may be worth while for that. And as soon as you see that you are making good progress, and that you have cut down your quantity of food, and are really eating in the Scientific Way, dismiss constipation from your mind forever; you have nothing more to do with it. Put your trust in that Principle within you which has the power to give you perfect health. Relate to God by your gratitude to the Principle of Life which is All Power, and go on your way rejoicing.

What about exercise? Everyone is the better for a little all-round use of the muscles every day, and the best way to get this is to do it by engaging in some form of play or amuse-ment. Get your exercise in the natural way — as recreation, not as a forced stunt for health's sake alone. Ride a horse or a bicycle, play tennis or tenpins, or toss a ball. Have some avocation like gardening in which you can spend an hour every day with pleasure and profit. There are a thousand ways in which you can get exercise enough to keep your body supple and your circulation good, and yet not fall into the rut of "exercising for your health." Exercise for fun or profit. Exercise because you are too healthy to sit still, and not because you wish to become healthy, or to remain so.

Are long continued fasts necessary? Seldom, if ever. The Principle of Health does not often require 20, 30, or 40 days to get ready for action. Under normal conditions, hunger will come in much less time. In most long fasts, the reason hunger does not come sooner is because it has been inhibited by the patient himself. He begins the fast with the FEAR if not actually with the hope that it will be many days before hunger comes. The literature he has read on the subject has prepared him to expect a long fast, and he is grimly determined to go to a finish, let the time be as long as it will. And the sub-conscious mind, under the influence of powerful and positive suggestion, suspends hunger.

When, for any reason, nature takes away your hunger, go cheerfully on with your usual work, and do not eat until she gives it back. No matter if it is two, three, ten days, or longer, you may be perfectly sure that when it is time for you to eat you will be hungry. And if you are cheerfully confident and keep your faith in health, you will suffer from no weakness or discomfort caused by abstinence.

When you are not hungry, you will feel stronger, happier, and more comfortable if you do not eat than you will if you do eat, no matter how long the fast. And if you live in the scientific way described in this book, you will never have to take long fasts, you will seldom miss a meal, and you will enjoy your meals more than ever before in your life. Get an earned hunger before you eat, and whenever you get an earned hunger, eat.

Chapter 17.
A Summary of the Science of Being Well

Health is perfectly natural functioning, normal living. There is a Principle of Life in the universe; it is the Living Substance, from which all things are made. This Living Substance permeates, penetrates, and fills the interspaces of the universe. In its invisible state it is in and through all forms, and yet all forms are made of it.

To illustrate: Suppose that a very fine and highly diffusible aqueous vapor should permeate and penetrate a block of ice. The ice is formed from living water and is living water in form, while the vapor is also living water, un-formed, permeating a form made from itself. This illustration will explain how Living Substance permeates all forms made from It. All life comes from It. It is all the life there is.

This Universal Substance is a thinking substance, and takes the form of its thought. The thought of a form, held by it, creates the form; and the thought of a motion causes the motion. It cannot help thinking, and so is forever creating. And it must move on toward fuller and more complete expression of itself. This means toward more complete life and more perfect functioning — and that means toward perfect health.

The power of the living substance must always be exerted toward perfect health. It is a force in all things making for perfect functioning.

All things are permeated by a power which makes for health.

A human being can relate himself to this power, and ally himself with it. He can also separate himself from it in his thoughts.

A human being is a form of this Living Substance, and has within him a Principle of Health. This Principle of Health, when in full constructive activity, causes all the involuntary functions of the human body to be perfectly performed.

A human being is a thinking substance, permeating a visible body, and the processes of his body are controlled by his thought.

When a person thinks only thoughts of perfect health, the internal processes of his body will be those of perfect health. A person's first step toward perfect health must be to form a conception of himself as perfectly healthy and as doing all things in the way and manner of a perfectly healthy person. Having formed this conception, he must relate himself to it in all his thoughts, and sever all thought relations with disease and weakness.

If he does this, and thinks his thoughts of health with positive FAITH, a person will cause the Principle of Health within him to become constructively active, and to heal all his diseases. He can receive additional power from the universal Principle of Life by faith, and he can acquire faith by looking to this Principle of Life with gratitude for the health it gives him. If a person will consciously accept the health which is being continually given to him by the Living Substance, and if he will be duly grateful for it, he will develop faith.

A person cannot think only thoughts of perfect health unless he performs the voluntary functions of life in a perfectly healthy manner. These voluntary functions are eating, drinking, breathing, and sleeping. If a person thinks only thoughts of health, has faith in health, and eats, drinks, breathes, and sleeps in a perfectly healthy way, he must have perfect health.

Health is the result of thinking and acting in a Certain Way, and if a sick person begins to think and act in this Way, the Principle of Health within him will come into constructive activity and heal all his diseases. This Principle of Heath is the same in all, and is related to the Life Principle of the universe. It is able to heal every disease, and will come into activity whenever a person thinks and acts in accordance with the Science of Being Well. Therefore, every person can attain perfect health.

THE END

BN Publishing

Improving People's Life

www.bnpublishing.com

We have Book Recommendations for you

Automatic Wealth: The Secrets of the Millionaire Mind--
Including: Acres of Diamonds, As a Man Thinketh, I Dare
you!, The Science of Getting Rich, The Way to Wealth, and
Think and Grow Rich [UNABRIDGED]
by Napoleon Hill, et al (CD-ROM)

Think and Grow Rich [MP3 AUDIO] [UNABRIDGED]
by Napoleon Hill, Jason McCoy (Narrator) (Audio CD)

As a Man Thinketh [UNABRIDGED]
by James Allen, Jason McCoy (Narrator) (Audio CD)

Your Invisible Power: How to Attain Your Desires by Letting
Your Subconscious Mind Work for You [MP3 AUDIO]
[UNABRIDGED] by Genevieve Behrend, Jason McCoy (Narrator)
(Audio CD)

Thought Vibration or the Law of Attraction in the Thought
World [MP3 AUDIO] [UNABRIDGED]
by William Walker Atkinson, Jason McCoy (Narrator)
(Audio CD)

Thought Vibration or the Law of Attraction in the Thought
World & Your Invisible Power (Paperback)

The Law of Success, Volume I: The Principles of Self-Mastery (Law of
Success, Vol 1) by Napoleon Hill (Paperback - Jun 20, 2006)

The Law of Success , Volume II & III: A Definite Chief Aim & Self
Confidence by Napoleon Hill (Paperback - Aug 15, 2006)

www.bnpublishing.com

Printed in the United States
72775LV00003B/111-238

9 789562 913607